SAY WHAT?

THE MANHANDLING OF THE CONSTITUTION

James A. Dueholm

PublishAmerica
Baltimore

First printing

At the specific preference of the author, PublishAmerica allowed this work to remain exactly as the author intended, verbatim, without editorial input.

ISBN: 1-4241-7392-2
PUBLISHED BY PUBLISHAMERICA, LLLP
www.publishamerica.com
Baltimore

Printed in the United States of America

For Pat, who was a sounding board without
ever sounding bored

Table of Contents

Introduction

This is a book about constitutional law, but it is not a scholarly work, nor am I a scholar. After graduation from Harvard Law School in 1967 and a year's clerkship with the Minnesota Supreme Court, I was a Minnesota real estate attorney for 34 years. Widely read in American history and biography, including judicial biography, and less so in constitutional law, I have no academic background in either field except for researching and writing occasional, conservative-oriented articles on constitutional law.

This, I believe, is good, for constitutional law is a discipline in which a lot of knowledge is a dangerous thing. As the domain of judges and academics, it dwells at length with Supreme Court cases and scholarly explication and analysis of those cases while spending little time with the Constitution, forgetting the truth-told-in-jest wisdom in Justice Robert Jackson's quip that the empty book shelves in the early Supreme Court "probably account for the high quality of the early opinions." Constitutional law has lost its way and forgot its first name.

The problem can be traced to two pernicious doctrines. The Supreme Court, abetted by liberal commentators, activists and special interest groups, has rejected original meaning or intent as a source of constitutional construction, opting instead for a vision of a "growing" or "evolving" Constitution. Then, as the Court pursued its vision, it developed a body of law that drifted ever farther from its constitutional moorings even as it claimed a self-fulfilling legitimacy and permanence under the doctrine of *stare decisis* or precedent. The fruit of this union of evolution and precedent is a modified and transformed Constitution that in several critical areas bears scant resemblance to that document as we received it from the Founders' pens.

It is a bitter fruit. As it amended the Constitution, the Supreme Court, often by a bare majority, set itself up as the arbiter of economic, cultural and social policy, assisting Congress in its unlawful expansion of power under the interstate commerce clause and depriving the American people of the power to preserve their cultural, social and religious heritage and values.

In this book, we will see how the Supreme Court planted this fruit, how it grew and spread, and what we might do to prune or uproot it. We will watch as the Court uses an eager acceptance of federal authority and a misreading of the interstate commerce clause to bless congressional grasp of illicit power. In exposing the Supreme Court's abuse of the commerce clause, which allows Congress to "regulate commerce among the states," we will prove, for what I believe is the first time, that the Court has for nearly 200 years used the wrong definition of "regulate" in applying this clause. We will follow the modern Court as it seizes a property-friendly misconstruction of the Fourteenth Amendment's due process clause, strips it of its property-protecting features, and employs it to support a liberal social and cultural agenda, nationalize abortion on demand and drive religion from the public square. By exploring the nature of the federal government through the "right" of secession, we will see how the Supreme Court has unconstitutionally subjected the states to federal power. We will see how the Court has unconstitutionally limited use of the death penalty and allowed colleges and professional schools to use racial and ethnic preferences in their admissions programs, and how it has misused the privilege against self-incrimination to hamstring police interrogations and keep relevant evidence from juries. Plunging into a current political thicket, we will expose the Senate Democrats' judicial filibuster as an unconstitutional abuse of power.

In the midst of these attacks on the Supreme Court, we will give the Court a breather. We will examine the Florida election fracas and discover that, contrary to conventional wisdom, the United States Supreme Court got it right while the Supreme Court of Florida violated both Florida law and the United States Constitution in an apparent attempt to make Al Gore president.

First, though, we will examine the concept of an evolving Constitution and the use of judicial precedent to repeat mistakes, for these unconstitutional foundations support most of the Supreme Court's misconstructions of the Constitution.

CHAPTER 1

Original Meaning and Precedent

This book argues among other things that the Supreme Court has unconstitutionally amended the interstate commerce, due process and religious establishment clauses of the Constitution. The argument makes two assumptions. First, that the Constitution means now what it meant when it was adopted, with that original meaning to be gleaned from the words of the Constitution, the intent of those—the Founders—who framed and ratified it, the purposes it was designed to serve, and the general public understanding of its powers, purposes and limitations when it was adopted. Second, that the doctrine of *stare decisis* or precedent, which the Supreme Court employs to repeat and expand its mistakes, is an illegitimate and unconstitutional tool in the development of constitutional law.

These assumptions are controversial. Since they underlie much of what we consider in succeeding chapters, discussion of the controversies is a good place to start.

JAMES A. DUEHOLM

Marshalling Support

Liberals don't like the doctrine of original meaning, often called originalism, as the source of constitutional construction. They belittle originalism as a concept that would hitch the modern world to a horse and buggy document. The Constitution, liberals argue, must grow with the times, with evolving powers adequate to meet the needs and address the problems of an ever-changing society and economy. The Constitution adopted by revolutionaries, they say, must be applied by evolutionaries, and they eagerly volunteer for the job. They believe they have John Marshall on their side.

John Marshall is the greatest judge that America has ever produced. Appointed Chief Justice of the United States in 1801, he was given the opportunity to construe a Constitution largely untouched by judicial hands, and he seized the opportunity with gusto, brilliance, flair, creativity, subtlety, a luminous and penetrating style, utter dominance of his fellow justices regardless of their political persuasion, and remorseless logic. In a series of decisions spanning his 34 years at the helm, he established the principle of judicial review, laid the legal foundations for a national economy, and assured that federal, as opposed to state, courts would construe the Constitution and determine the scope of federal powers. In words that Thomas Jefferson begrudgingly applied to Alexander Hamilton, Marshall was a legion unto himself, and he drove his opponents crazy. Responding in anger and frustration to a Marshall opinion, eccentric, dyspeptic Virginia Congressman John Randolph of Roanoke said that the opinion was "wrong, wrong, all wrong–but no one can tell how or wherein." The Liberty Bell cracked as it tolled Marshall's death in 1835, never to clang again. It's no wonder liberals want to use Marshall to make their case for an evolving Constitution, and they believe that his opinion in *McCulloch v Maryland* does just that.[1]

In the 1790s Congress created the Bank of the United States over the strong protests of Jefferson, who believed it was a foundation block in a big federal government structure. When the bank reached the end of its 20 year life in 1811, the Jeffersonians, in power since 1801, let it lapse. Those in power soon decided that it was maybe a useful device after all, so in 1816 Congress, at the urging of President James Madison, created the Second Bank of the United States. Even though Madison was the Jeffersonian second only to Jefferson himself, strict constructionist Jeffersonians attacked the bank as an unconstitutional exercise of federal power. There was, they said, no provision in the Constitution expressly empowering Congress to charter a bank. They acknowledged that Article I, Section 8 of the Constitution authorized Congress to "make all laws necessary and proper" to implement its other powers, but argued that necessary in this provision meant absolutely necessary, and that a bank was not absolutely necessary to implement any of Congress' enumerated powers.

In *McCulloch*, Marshall upheld the constitutionality of the bank as an appropriate means of implementing the powers entrusted to Congress, including the powers to collect taxes, borrow money, regulate commerce, support the armed services, and wage war. Stressing that, in a government meant to endure for the ages, the Constitution could not possibly catalog all of the devices Congress could employ to implement its powers, he said that necessary did not mean absolutely necessary, but only convenient, with Congress empowered to adopt any means calculated to exercise its enumerated powers. In the course of his opinion, Marshall uttered what are probably the most famous words in constitutional law. "We must never forget," he said, "that it is a Constitution that we are expounding."

These words are grist for the evolutionists' mill. The great man himself, they say, recognizes that the Constitution cannot be frozen in time, but must grow and evolve in response to what Justice Oliver Wendell Holmes called the "felt necessities of the time."

This reliance on Marshall is misplaced. Liberals cite Marshall to support evolution in the powers of government—for example, to grow the interstate commerce and due process clauses—but Marshall in *McCulloch* speaks to the means of exercising power, not to the powers themselves. Flexibility among means is not a brief for expanding ends. Marshall agrees, acknowledging in *McCulloch* that "the powers of government are limited and are not to be transcended" even as he insists that the Constitution must be read to "allow discretion with respect to the means by which the powers it confers are to be carried into execution."[2]

Justice Holmes is second only to Marshall in the judicial pantheon, but as a reed for the evolutionists to lean on, he is as slender as Marshall. The necessities of the time can be met by a Constitution tied to its ancient moorings. The primary source of Congressional power is the interstate commerce clause. While the Supreme Court has, as we shall see in Chapter 2, stretched that clause far beyond the breaking point, the clause if properly construed can respond to the needs and demands of a national and international economy, and the states can deal with the rest. For example, as discussed below, the Endangered Species Act and the Supreme Court's nationalization of the Bill of Rights are unconstitutional, but the states could protect endangered species and could adopt their own bills of rights, as most if not all of them have in fact done. To the extent federal protection of speech and press were needed to support interstate communication and media industries and facilities, Congress could provide it under the interstate commerce clause. The evolutionists' real objection to a static Constitution is not that modern society presents problems impervious to government response under a hidebound Constitution. Their concern is that, in many cases, the first and only responders would have to be the states. This concern reflects the liberals' desire to entrust their agenda to power at the farthest possible remove from popular control; federal legislation is better than state legislation, and federal judicial legislation is best of all.

The real absurdity of the evolutionists' position is exposed by considering it in the context of their support for *stare decisis* or precedent. The post-New Deal Supreme Court's attachment to the idea of an expanding Constitution has allowed it to consistently misapply the Constitution. If originalists achieve a majority on the Supreme Court, the mostly-liberal evolutionists would no doubt seek to preserve their easily won gains by contending that the doctrine of judicial precedent has hardened the Supreme Court's accumulated misdeeds into settled, unchangeable law. Stripped to its skivvies, the evolutionists' position is that, in construing the Constitution, the mistakes of those who did not frame or adopt the Constitution count for more than the intent of those who did. As we used to say on the farm, that don't make much sense.

Even if there were prudential or reasoned bases for a malleable Constitution, the squishiness could not be squared with the words of the Constitution, which sets its face firmly against judicial or legislative expansion of its powers.

A document can be amended by change, deletion or addition. The Constitution is amended to the extent it "grows" to increase or transform its powers. The growth is amendment even if it occurs by stealth and, as Lincoln would say, by "littles"—gradual expansions or transformations which add up over time. And it has occurred. Sometimes the stealth amendments are enacted by the Supreme Court alone, as in the case of the due process and religious establishment clauses, and sometimes by the Supreme Court in cahoots with Congress, as in the case of the interstate commerce clause. These amendments are unconstitutional.

Article V of the Constitution allows amendment only by action of two thirds of both houses of Congress and three fourths of the states. The Supreme Court has no authority, either alone or in concert with Congress, to amend the Constitution .

Article V has a further significance, as an expression of intent. The Constitution cannot easily be changed, and intentionally so. In the 214 years since the first ten amendments were adopted as a block, the Constitution has only been amended 17 times. The amendment provisions embody original meaning, insisting that the Constitution remain as adopted unless and until, and only to the extent that, it is changed in response to strong political and popular demand expressed in joint supermajority action by Congress and the states.

The originalist expression of the amending provisions is hammered home by the Tenth Amendment of the Constitution, which states that "powers not delegated to the United States by the Constitution…are reserved to the States respectively or to the people."

Evolutionists argue that the Tenth Amendment is just a truism that does not impose a new restriction on federal power, but simply confirms the obvious limitation implicit in a government of specifically enumerated powers. Perhaps so, but the amendment does confirm the nature of that implicit limitation. The Tenth Amendment is America's first no-growth initiative, dividing power between the federal government and the states as of 1791, when the amendment was adopted, and freezing federal power as of that date. Unlike the federal government, states have unlimited sovereign power, unbound by time, circumstances or subject matter, with all the authority needed at any time to meet the needs and demands of governance. The Tenth Amendment obviously divides the universe of power as of 1791, and not as of some later or ever-changing date, limiting the federal government to its constitutional powers as understood at that time, and assigning all other powers, including all non-federal powers needed then or in the future to respond to unknown circumstances or to address emerging needs, to the states as the residuary legatees of sovereign power.

The evolutionists' dismissal of the Tenth Amendment ignores its context as well as its words.

Young Abe Lincoln was an avid fan of *Aesop's Fables*, endlessly reading them aloud to his cousin Dennis Hanks. Once Dennis, exasperated, said "them's all lies Abe."

"Mighty fine lies, Denny," Abe replied, "mighty fine lies." If the Tenth Amendment is a truism, it is a mighty fine truism, as confirmed by the company it keeps.

The Tenth Amendment is the last of the amendments adopted as a package and known as the Bill of Rights. In addition to the Tenth Amendment, and among other things, the Bill of Rights guarantees freedom of speech, press, assembly and religion; confers protections from unreasonable searches and seizures; imposes procedural safeguards in criminal proceedings; and prohibits cruel and unusual punishment.

Widely discussed when the Constitution was before the states for ratification, promised to reluctant state delegations as an inducement to ratify the Constitution, sponsored by James Madison, the Father of the Constitution, sent to the states by the first Congress, and ratified during Washington's first term, the Bill of Rights embodies the Founders' and the founding generation's most cherished restrictions on federal power. And the Tenth Amendment is right up there with freedom of speech.

Here, then, is where Marshall's famous dictum really applies. The debates at the Constitutional Convention, heated resistance to the Constitution during the ratification process, and insistence upon and adoption of the Bill of Rights all confirm that the founding generation was probably more concerned with what the Constitution didn't do than what it did. And the Constitution's restrictions, implicit and express, like the constitutional powers, were to endure for all time (or at least until changed in accordance with the amendment provisions). Given the critical, document-defining role of the restrictions in the adoption and ratification of the Constitution, it is in observing the limits of federal power, even more than in allowing flexibility in its exercise, that "we must never forget that it is a Constitution that we are expounding."

There is one apparent exception to original meaning, but it is only apparent, not real. The Eighth Amendment bans "cruel and unusual punishment." This ban by its very nature embodies a community standard. A time-frozen standard would be at odds with the purpose of the ban, reducing it to an historical relic as evolving sensibilities reject the use or lessen the severity of once-common punishments. In this instance, original meaning is an evolving standard. (As we will see in Chapter 7, the Supreme Court has bungled the determination and application of that standard in its capital punishment cases, but that's a different matter.)

The importance of originalism should not be overstated. It is the beginning, not the end, of constitutional construction, and it is not an Easy Button to be used to summon decision in specific cases. For one thing, many provisions of the Constitution, including the interstate commerce and due process clauses, are stated in broad terms, and neither originalism nor any other principle of construction will effortlessly determine their scope or provide an automatic basis for decision. For another, originalists concede that even static powers can respond to the times. There is a fine line between an unconstitutional expansion of federal power, on one hand, and the legitimate exercise of existing power in response to changing circumstances, on the other. As Chief Justice Charles Evans Hughes said in upholding Minnesota's mortgage moratorium statute during the Great Depression, emergency does not create power, but it may create an occasion for its exercise.[3] Originalism does, however, provide an historical and analytical framework for uncovering the governing purposes which guide the application and establish the scope of government powers.

Original meaning should be distinguished from strict construction and original intent, two other doctrines of constitutional construction used to restrict judicial or legislative expansion of federal power, for original meaning is sometimes confused with these other doctrines. Strict constructionists insist upon a narrow or literal reading of the words of the Constitution, which is difficult in view of the intentionally vague and even opaque formulation of federal powers in the Constitution, and doesn't work in practice. The Constitution refers in four places to land and naval forces of the United States, so read literally the Constitution would not empower Congress to raise or equip an air force or subject its members to military law, and would not give the president control over the air force in his role as commander in chief. The First Amendment protects "speech" and "press," which under their 1791 meanings would not include a lot of modern media and communication facilities. Technological devices for snooping in homes do not fit well with the Constitution's restrictions on unreasonable searches and seizures. Congressional power to "coin" money could be read to exclude a right to issue paper currency. As Marshall showed in *McCulloch*, strict construction would not allow flexibility in adapting means to ends, and as we will see in discussing *Gibbons v. Ogden* in Chapter 2, a strict reading of the Constitution would allow the states to throttle interstate and foreign commerce. Examples could be multiplied.

The original intent school of construction focuses narrowly on the intent of those who framed and adopted the Constitution. While relevant, such intent is not adequate as the basis for constitutional construction, for the specific statements of Madison or Hamilton or others may or may not reflect the collective understanding of those who adopted and ratified the Constitution. For example, in the *Federalist Papers* Madison claims that taxes raised under Congress' seemingly unlimited power to levy taxes can only be used to service other enumerated powers in the Constitution,[4] but the Constitution cannot fairly be read to support this claim. The text and context of a constitutional provision, its background and history, the purpose it was designed to serve and the general public understanding of the provision when it was proposed and ratified are better guides to meaning than the specific intent of individuals.

In determining original meaning, words, if clear, are the gold standard. The Fourteenth Amendment in its various provisions protects "citizens" and "persons" without qualification. The principal purpose of this 1868 amendment was to protect the recently-freed slaves, but its words cannot reasonably be limited to Blacks, let alone ex-slaves—all of whom would be dead in about 75 years—any more than the Thirteenth Amendment, outlawing slavery, could be read to allow enslavement of Whites, Latinos, Asians or American Indians on the grounds that the only people freed by the amendment were Blacks. There is in any event no real tension between the principal purpose of these amendments and the scope of the language. Legislators in enacting a statute or proposing a constitutional amendment can target a particular group or class without excluding others.

Since the New Deal, the Supreme Court has used its vision of a growing Constitution to unconstitutionally expand the interstate commerce clause and to misapply the due process and religious establishment clauses. Feeding and building on themselves, the decisions in these areas have produced a large and growing body of entrenched "law" that claims justification and demands permanence under the doctrine of *stare decisis* or precedent—the principle that a court is bound by its prior cases, whether right or wrong. If precedent does indeed protect and expand this body of law, which aggressively rejects originalism, then originalism is of only academic interest. Originalists must therefore confront precedent.

Two Wrongs Make a Right

The doctrine of precedent is generally described as the policy of a court to follow its prior decisions. As so stated, this formulation gives a veneer of reason to an unreasonable doctrine. For a court, using a correct prior decision as the basis for a later decision is convenient but not necessary; one need not justify the conclusion that $2 + 2$ equals 4 by pointing out that millions of others have reached the same conclusion. As a source of law, the real function of precedent is to repeat and expand mistakes—to uphold a prior case that concludes that $2 + 2$ equals 5, and to use that case in similar and not-so-similar cases in which $2 + 2$ equals 6 or 7 or more.

When applied to statutes and constitutions, this judicial policy of embracing error intentionally amends the document which the court is supposedly applying. If a court mistakenly construes a statute or constitution, it unwittingly amends the document. If it follows that decision knowing it to be wrong, error becomes scofflaw as the court intentionally and permanently alters that document by expansion, deletion or modification. In his Cooper Union Speech, Lincoln said that the South reversed the moral order, calling not the sinners but the saints to repentance, when it charged that the North would be responsible if the South seceded because the North refused to yield to Southern demands for slavery expansion. In knowingly repeating an earlier error, a court also defies conventional morality, insisting that two wrongs do indeed make a right.

Two wrongs become three wrongs when the Supreme Court wilfully repeats a misreading of the Constitution. Article VII of the Constitution stipulates that "judicial Officers…of the United States…shall be bound by oath or affirmation to support this Constitution." Justices who decide that a prior mistake trumps constitutional text betray this oath.

Mistaken construction of a statute or constitutional provision not only amends the document, but often constitutes after-the-fact fraud in the inducement, producing a law which could not have been enacted in its judicially altered form. Take the Michigan case permitting racial preferences in university and graduate school admissions, for example. When he pressed for passage of the 1964 Civil Rights Act, Senator Hubert Humphrey assured skeptics that if the act was ever read to permit racial preferences, he would eat the paper it was written on. Death has spared Humphrey a fiber-rich diet, but his assurances suggest that a statute embodying the provisions of the Michigan decision would not have passed in 1964, and it almost certainly could not be enacted even now. Similarly, it is safe to say that those who proposed and ratified the interstate commerce, due process and establishment clauses would not have done so, or would have done so in a different form, if they had known what the Supreme Court would do with them.

The problem grows worse with time. As a couple of examples will show, a court, having embedded an error in the law, builds upon the error, using it to decide similar and not-so-similar cases and developing a self-absorbed corpus of judicial law while increasingly losing sight of the statute or constitution that it is supposedly applying.

In *Everson v. Board of Education*, the Supreme Court adopted Jefferson's wall of separation metaphor as the standard the Court would apply in determining whether states have improperly established religion.[5] As discussed below, that decision is wrong. Since *Everson*, the Court has consistently struck down state laws that, in the view of at least five justices, aid or endorse religion. In doing so the Court, grappling with the practical application of the wall of separation metaphor, has developed a head-scratching body of law that has produced bickering on the Court, sowed confusion and consternation among commentators, and trivialized the establishment clause.

The apex—or nadir, depending on your point of view—was reached in *County of Allegheny v. ACLU*, a 1989 decision that consumed lots of trees to conclude that the establishment clause allowed the public display of a menorah but not a creche.[6] Here is the Supreme Court's own introduction to the welter of opinions in the case:

Blackmun, J announced the judgment of the Court and delivered the opinion of the Court with respect to Parts III-A, IV and V, in which Brennan, Marshall, Stevens and O'Connor…joined, an opinion with respect to Parts I and II in which Stevens and O'Connor joined, an opinion with respect to Part III-B in which Stevens joined, an opinion with respect to Part VII in which O'Connor joined, and an opinion with respect to Part VI. O'Connor, J filed an opinion concurring in part and concurring in the judgment, in Part II of which Brennan and Stevens joined. Brennan J filed an opinion concurring in part and dissenting in part, in which Marshall and Stevens joined. Stevens, J filed an opinion concurring in part and dissenting in part, in which Brennan and Marshall joined. Kennedy, J filed an opinion concurring in part and dissenting in part, in which Rehnquist, White and Scalia joined.

This reads like a *Saturday Night Live* parody, but I am not making it up.

This introduction suggests a court that has lost its way, and the opinions that taken together speak for the 5-4 majority second the suggestion. The Court cites itself over 100 times; it repeatedly mentions the Maccabees; it explores the origins and significance of Christmas, Chanukah and Christmas trees; it cites the Bible and the Talmud, the *Encyclopedia of Religion*, articles on Christmas and general articles and books on religion; it endlessly cites and examines what "we"—a decidedly royal we—have said in prior decisions about the meaning and application of the establishment clause. In all these pages, however, the Constitution as originally understood is mentioned only briefly and dismissively, with the Court indicating that while "in the early days of the Republic" the establishment clause had meant such and so, the Court had long since and repeatedly rejected that meaning.

The Court's privacy cases display the same runaway truck pattern as its establishment clause cases.

Connecticut law outlawed contraceptives. In *Griswold v. Connecticut*, the Supreme Court concluded that the law was unconstitutional, but struggled to justify the conclusion.[7] Unable to find support for its decision in any provisions of the Constitution, desperate to establish a principle that couldn't be used to protect property rights—the Court expressly refused to base its decision on the principle established in an earlier property-friendly case—the Court found a right of privacy in "the penumbras, formed by emanations" from specific provisions of the Bill of Rights. According to the dictionary, a "penumbra" is a shadow and an "emanation" is an emission, so the Court finds constitutional law in the shadows of emissions from the Bill of Rights. This is pretty thin gruel, akin to a Stephen Douglas position that Lincoln said reminded him of a soup brewed from the shadow of a pigeon that had died of starvation.

The soup was thin, but it was sustenance enough for the Supreme Court. *Griswold* allowed the Court to slip the surly bonds of the Constitution. Penumbras and emanations and the nettlesome Constitution itself were left in the dust as the Court, citing itself, discovered in *Roe v. Wade* that the right of privacy included a constitutional right to abortion on demand for the first six months of pregnancy,[8] and then confirmed a besieged *Roe* in *Planned Parenthood v. Casey*.[9]

The *Casey* Court articulated the right of privacy by exclaiming that "at the heart of liberty is the right to define one's own concept of existence, of meaning, of the universe and of the meaning of human life." This is gibberish. What on earth does it mean? What possible guide to decision does it provide? What conceivable source can it claim in any fairly-read provision of the Constitution? In 27 years a previously unknown right found lurking in shadows formed by emissions has morphed into a metaphysical musing whose meaning is known but to God and five justices of the United States Supreme Court. And the Constitution is nowhere to be seen.

Casey not only stumps philosophers. It announces a doctrine of super precedent, a category of cases in which the Court is even more reluctant than usual to reverse itself, making a bad doctrine worse.

Roe v. Wade has been widely criticized by commentators on both the right and the left.[10] It has been pilloried as judicial legislation that was wrong on the law, embittered cultural and political debate by provoking impotent fury on the right and an addiction to judicial fiat on the left, and converted formerly staid judicial confirmation proceedings into venomous, rancorous forums for selecting lifetime legislators. (In Chapter 3, we will see that *Roe*'s low esteem is well-deserved.) A court intent on upholding *Roe* had a tall order, but in *Casey* the Supreme Court, upholding *Roe* in a 5-4 decision, gave it the old college try.

Supreme Court opinions are ordinarily written by a single justice, but the opinion of the Court in *Casey* was jointly authored by Justices Sandra Day O'Connor, Anthony Kennedy and David Souter. As the opinion develops, it becomes apparent that the three have sought strength in numbers as they sound an uncertain trumpet for *Roe*. They suggest that they might have decided differently as an original matter, offer *Roe* only tepid endorsement on the merits, admit that it may have been in error, and defend it primarily by appealing to precedent and the Court's institutional integrity. The opinion begins with an extended but traditional defense of the doctrine of precedent. Then, noting the "intensely divisive controversy" involving *Roe*, the Court said that it would "subvert its legitimacy beyond any question" if it were to "surrender under fire" to this controversy. With this background, the Court announces its doctrine of super precedent. The Court has a special duty, it said, to uphold a case which resolves an intensely divisive controversy because "such a case has a dimension that calls the contending sides of a national controversy to end their division by accepting a common mandate rooted in the Constitution." *Roe*, it concluded, is just such a case.

As a device for resolving a divisive national debate, *Casey* is in bad company. Before his inauguration as president on March 4, 1857, James Buchanan had been in touch with members of the Supreme Court, and in his inaugural address he urged his countrymen to accept the Supreme Court's upcoming decision on slavery expansion, whatever it might be. Two days later, in *Dred Scott v. Sandford*, the Court decided that the black man had no rights that the white man was bound to respect, and that Congress had no constitutional authority to prohibit slavery in the territories.[11] Buchanan and the Court thought that the Court had resolved the festering, never-ending, union-rending debate over slavery expansion. They were wrong. Judging by the continuing debate over abortion restrictions, it appears that the *Casey* justices have been no more successful.

Casey's super precedent concept is troubling for a number of reasons beyond its apparent failure as a peacemaker. It exalts the Court's reputation and institutional standing above the

Constitution and the legitimate political processes of a democratic society. It strengthens precedent when it should be weakening it, since it is "intensely divisive controversies" that are most apt to have pushed the Court over the line dividing law from policy. Worst of all, in endorsing a mistake because it refereed a political tussle, it acknowledges that the mistake was itself political.

The Court has no precedent for this super precedent. On the contrary, the Court acknowledges that it has reversed both of the other decisions that had generated *Roe* level controversy. *Casey* stands alone, a solitary, newly-minted exemplar of the proposition that while the Court will ordinarily hug its mistakes, it reserves its most fervent embrace for its catastrophic mistakes.

Casey and the Supreme Court's other Constitution-amending confirmations of past mistakes could perhaps be justified if the Court invariably followed precedent, for it could then plead that the devil made it do it. It frequently reverses itself, however, both in specific cases, as in its 2002 decision requiring juries to decide whether the death penalty is called for,[12] its 2003 decision overturning state sodomy laws,[13] and its 2005 decision outlawing execution of juveniles,[14] and in undoing long-established, well-settled bodies of law, as in the Warren Court's rejection of the 58 year old separate but equal doctrine[15] and the Roosevelt Court's scuttling of a decades long body of property-protective law.[16] Souter and Kennedy, who sang the praises of precedent in *Casey*, joined in the Court's flip-flops on jury decisions, sodomy laws and juvenile execution. We will see in Chapter 7 that the Court eagerly, frequently and quickly abandons precedent in its crusade to limit the death penalty, with Kennedy and Souter among the crusaders. In other chapters we will see many other conservative precedents fall prey to a liberal agenda. The Court, by deciding whether or not to stand by an earlier mistake, is consciously deciding, as a matter of policy, whether or not to amend the Constitution, and this is certainly what it did in *Casey*. And the mistakes it stands by are its liberal mistakes.

The Court's inconstancy on precedent not only highlights its Constitution-amending, liberal-serving roles; for interest groups, as for the Court itself, it makes precedent the first refuge of scoundrels, as partisans on both sides plump for precedent when it serves their purposes and reject it when it doesn't. When the *New York Times* editorial page turns to pending or recently decided Supreme Court decisions, outcome will trump all other considerations, as evidenced by a few examples. When the Supreme Court allowed Georgia Democrats to divide a minority-majority district into two Democrat-leaning districts on the grounds that Republicans are not a protected class, the *Times* cheered the outcome while expressing a nagging concern that two could play the game of creating districts for partisan advantage. Sure enough, when the Republicans played that game in Texas and Pennsylvania, the *Times* wanted the courts to step in. In an editorial written as the Supreme Court considered the backyard marijuana case, the *Times* urged the Court to hold that Congress has no power to prohibit non-commercial cultivation of marijuana for personal use, but to do so in a way that did not weaken the Court's expansive reading of the interstate commerce clause, which has proved so useful in advancing the liberal agenda. And of course the *Times* insists upon permanence for *Roe* and other stars in the liberal judicial firmament while it attacks inconvenient precedent in its crusade against the death penalty. The *Times*' March 2, 2005 issue displays side-by-side evidence of this precedential opportunism and liberal world view, as one editorial cheers the Supreme Court's reversal on juvenile executions while another urges the Court to use its establishment clause precedents to banish the Ten Commandments from the public square. The *Times* reflects and expresses the left's scorn for a principled use of precedent.

The members of the Supreme Court have no special qualifications for their self-appointed role as legislators or, as in *Casey*, super legislators. They need not have any academic or judicial background, or any particular knowledge of American history or constitutional law. They are apt to be appointed because of friendship with or support of the president, or political availability, or support of special interests, or perceived ability to avoid a Senate filibuster. As Justice Robert Jackson noted, the Supreme Court is infallible because it is final, not final because it is infallible. In upholding *Roe* despite obvious misgivings, the *Casey* Court elected to allow a mistake made by three accidental occupants of the Supreme Court in 1973—*Roe* was a 7-2 decision—to forever decide a matter of policy affecting 300 million people.

How did we come to this pass, with the Supreme Court amending the Constitution as it sees fit and its partisans and opponents cheering or jeering to the echo? Why do judges, alone among public officials, repeat and multiply their mistakes and then brag about it, as the *Casey* Court did, asserting that mere error is not an adequate basis to overturn a precedent? Why do Supreme Court justices use mistakes to betray their oath of office? To paraphrase Justice Holmes, a page of history explains volumes of illogic. And if we read that page carefully, we will see where the courts went awry in using their mistakes as a source of law in statutory and constitutional construction.

In late old England and early New England there were few statutes and no constitutions. Courts were forced to resolve disputes involving personal injuries and other non-contractual wrongs (torts), contracts, maritime and commercial transactions and other matters. In the absence of controlling legislative or constitutional authority, the decisions often reflected policy choices, as in the selection of the tort doctrines of negligence, fellow worker and assumption of risk to protect and promote industry, and the development of negotiable instrument rules to create a free market in the sales of notes and bonds.

Over time, courts followed earlier decisions in identical and similar cases, applying and expanding principles announced in those decisions. Gradually, a corpus of judge-made law, known as the common law, emerged to govern conduct and transactions in most areas of human endeavor.

In the development of the common law, precedent served a number of purposes. Citing an earlier case in the same or similar circumstances provided a shortcut to decision, avoiding the need to decide each case anew. Consistent decisions over time reduced litigation by discouraging disputes in settled areas of law and allowed parties to commercial transactions to conduct their affairs with a reasonable expectation that the rules of the game would not change. Most importantly, in the absence of a controlling statute or constitutional provision, a decision in an unlitigated area established law when it was delivered and provided a source of law for future decisions on the same or similar facts.

Accustomed to the uses of precedent in the development of the common law, American lawyers and judges adopted them lock, stock and barrel to the construction of statutes and constitutions. And here is where they went astray—they should have adopted lock and stock and left the barrel behind.

The lock and stock are use of precedent as a shortcut to decision and as a protector of justifiable reliance. If a court properly construes a statutory or constitutional provision, it can rightly use its decision as a convenient tool to decide identical or similar cases as they arise. If the court misapplies the statute or constitution it can correct its error in such a way as to protect the rights and interests of those who have acted in reliance on the mistake. If it were to reverse *Roe*, for example, the Supreme Court could make its decision effective in, say, 12 months, and courts mindful of those who have relied on an error often make their corrective decisions prospective only.[17]

The barrel is the use of precedent as law and source of law. In common law, as we have seen, a decision in an unplowed field established law, and it could be and often was based on policy grounds. In these circumstances, there could be no "wrong" decision by objective standards, any more than a legislator's vote can be called wrong by such standards.

The situation is different when a court construes a statutory or constitutional provision. Here the decision is not law but an understanding of law, and if a court becomes aware of an earlier mistake it should correct it, not repeat it and expand it as a source of law

Casey and other supporters of error as a source of constitutional law claim that a too-eager correction of error will produce a Constitution in constant flux as the composition of the Supreme Court changes and its outlook swings back and forth. But this assumes that the Court will make frequent errors or will often push the envelope, and will not learn from its mistakes. Presumably the Court will not make frequent errors. It should be wary of pushing the envelope, and it would be a good thing if fear of a changing balance on the Court discourages it from doing so; the lesson that *Casey* should have taken from *Roe* is not that the Court needs to build a firewall around its own fires, but rather that it shouldn't play with matches. As for learning from its mistakes, in view of the attacks on *Roe* from right and left, the advance of medical science and knowledge of fetal development since *Roe* was decided, and the firestorm that *Roe* ignited, my guess is that if *Casey* had overturned *Roe* a reconstituted court would have been reluctant to reenter the fray. The same would likely be true of other controversial decisions. An occasional yo-yoing of decisions prompted by a willingness to correct error is in any event preferable to uncontrolled and uncontrollable legislation by judicial fiat.

The Supreme Court's erroneous constructions of the interstate commerce, due process and religious establishment clauses are long-standing and well-established. The apologists for those constructions would no doubt argue that the age, growth and acceptance of long-followed errors give them a legitimacy not enjoyed by an occasional error. As we have seen, the Supreme Court itself has not bought this argument. Now about 60, most of the modern Court's misconstructions are roughly the same age as the property-friendly body of law interred by the Roosevelt Supreme Court and the string of separate-but-equal decisions rejected by *Brown v. Board of Education*, while the right of privacy is a youngish 40, and *Roe v. Wade*, its most misbegotten son, is barely 30. If anything, a mistaken body of law deserves less protection than a solitary error, for as we have seen, a mistake-based corpus of law departs ever farther from the Constitution as it ages and grows. Besides, time and conventional wisdom do not confer power. As Justice Holmes said in the Taxicab case, a mistaken application of governing law is "an unconstitutional assumption of powers by the Courts of the United States which no lapse of time or respectable array of opinion should hesitate to make us correct," and he said it in objecting to a long line of cases stretching back 86 years.[18]

Constitutional misconstruction is, in particular, "assumption of power" that should find no sanctuary in time or array of opinion. If a court misconstrues a statute, the mistake can be corrected by a legislative majority—though that is often easier said than done. It is nearly impossible to muster the supermajorities of Congress and the states needed to amend the Constitution to undo a wrongful decision of the Supreme Court. In nearly 220 years, it has only been done twice, in the Eleventh Amendment, depriving federal courts of jurisdiction in actions by citizens of one state against another state, and the Sixteenth Amendment, legalizing the federal income tax. (The Fourteenth Amendment overturned *Dred Scott*, but that amendment did not really achieve the willing support of two thirds of Congress or three fourths of the states, for several Southern congressional delegations were excluded from the Congress that proposed it in 1866, and several Southern states were forced to ratify the amendment in order to gain readmission to Congress.) A self-correcting Supreme Court is the only defense against judicial tyranny, the only way to assure that the mistake of a temporary, accidentally-assembled majority of the Supreme Court does not forever preempt the political processes of a democratic society.

In common law, decision as a source of law promotes a healthy, orderly, responsive development of rules to live and act by. In statutory and constitutional construction, the use of error as a source of law is both malignant and metastatic, and in constitutional construction it is inoperable by all but judicial surgeons. It is time to excise the cancer. It is time for the *Casey* metaphysicians and their like-minded brethren to heal themselves.

CHAPTER 2

The Interstate Commerce Clause— Power Run Amok

The Constitution empowers Congress to "regulate commerce among the several states." In the hands of Congress and the federal courts, this interstate commerce clause has become The Little Engine That Could, pulling federal power to unimagined, outrageous, unconstitutional heights. How this happened, and what to do about it, requires context. And that begins with the little steamboat that shooed the other steamboats from its pond.

Robert Fulton v. John Marshall

Robert Fulton had a sweet deal, a state-minted monopoly. His competitors were steamed, and as Americans have done ever since in ever-greater numbers, they went to court. The nature and location of Fulton's monopoly, the personalities involved and the enduring economy- and power-altering influence of the decision in the case combine to tell a compelling story. The story features Chief Justice John Marshall, Daniel Webster, Cornelius Vanderbilt, the inventor of the steamboat, the chancellor of New York, the picturesque appeal of the pre-industrial water-borne coastal trade, and a cat fight between New York and New Jersey. The central player in the story was the then-unlitigated interstate commerce clause, which is best seen in its constitutional setting.

The colonies that won the Revolutionary War were banded together in a loose-knit, unwieldy, makeshift coalition. The war was a near-run thing, the father of victory more an irresolute England and a helpful France than a resolute union of colonies. During the war the colonies sought a more permanent and effective union under a compact called the Articles of Confederation, but Maryland opposition delayed formation of the new union until 1781, near the end of the war.

The new government didn't work. As Dan Rather might say, problems emerged faster than a race horse from a starting gate. Taxes could only be levied through the states, and states could and did ignore or defy levies. Executive power was weak, vested in a president appointed by Congress for a very limited term. States could and did impose duties and taxes at their borders, impeding the conduct and frustrating the development of interstate and foreign commerce.

Congress, recognizing the defects of the Articles but unwilling to scrap them, called a convention of delegates instructed to consider amendments of, but not an alternative to, the Articles. When the delegates assembled in Philadelphia in May, 1787, they promptly defied their instructions, deciding as one of their first orders of business to propose a new constitution. Sweltering in the dog days of summer, struggling with indifferent and frequently truant delegates and delegations, the delegates deliberated, dithered, bickered and compromised for nearly four months. Finally, on September 17, 1787, the delegates signed a proposed constitution authored primarily by

Gouverneur Morris, a peg-legged libertine from New York, and sent it to the states for ratification. It had not been easy, with success achieved only by flexibility, imagination, log-rolling, compromise and participation by the likes of Washington, Franklin, Hamilton, Madison and Morris.

The job wasn't done yet, of course; the proposed constitution had to be ratified by the states. By its terms, the constitution would become effective upon the ratifying states as soon as nine states ratified, but as a practical matter the new government was a no-go without New York and Virginia, the biggest and dominant states. Resistance was widespread, but was particularly strong in these two states. In New York, Governor George Clinton and his faction, intent on retaining their power and position, fiercely opposed ratification, and they elected a majority of delegates to New York's ratification convention, out-polling Hamilton's pro-constitution coalition. In Virginia, Patrick Henry and other small government advocates rallied against ratification.

The pro-constitution forces fought back. Madison and Hamilton, with a little help from John Jay of New York, penned and widely distributed a series of pro-constitution essays, known collectively as *The Federalist Papers*, that were effective then and remain a classic today. In the end, Virginia became the tenth state to ratify the proposed constitution, and New York, unwilling to be left out in the cold, followed suit. On April 30, 1789, in New York City, George Washington was inaugurated as president under the new constitution, with 11 states on board. (North Carolina and Rhode Island joined within a year, bringing all 13 original colonies within the fold.)

Aware of the fiscal roadblocks the states had erected at their boundaries and mindful that the nation's fledgling interstate and foreign commerce might not grow and thrive without federal protection and control, the Constitution restricts state power to tax imports and exports and empowers Congress to "regulate commerce with foreign nations and among the several states."

Read strictly, however, these provisions create a dangerous loophole. The states cannot tax interstate or foreign commerce, but the Constitution does not by its terms impose any other restrictions on the states' power to regulate this commerce. Since the Constitution seemingly imposes no non-fiscal restraints on state power over commerce, why can't the states, as sovereign powers, regulate and restrict this commerce? Why can't they, for example, grant benefits or impose restrictions that favor local commerce at the expense of interstate or foreign commerce? Nobody really knew whether the interstate commerce clause restricted the states. Well, not quite nobody. John Marshall knew.

Which brings us back to Robert Fulton and his monopoly.

New York state granted steam-boat inventor Fulton and Robert Livingston, the chancellor of New York, the exclusive right for several years to operate fire and steam driven vessels on the waters of New York state. They licensed Aaron Ogden to operate a ferry between New York City and Elizabethtown Port, New Jersey. Thomas Gibbons held a navigational license under a 1793 federal coastal trading law. Using this license, Gibbons employed Cornelius Vanderbilt to operate a ferry service in competition with Ogden. Born in 1794, a budding businessman at 16, the uneducated, aggressive, ruthless, resourceful Vanderbilt was building an empire that would make him, at his death in 1877, the richest man in the world.

Meanwhile, New Jersey joined the fray, enacting a law fining anyone who obtained a New York judgment enforcing the New York monopoly. Emotions ran high. Undeterred, Ogden obtained an injunction against Gibbons from the New York courts. Gibbons appealed to John Marshall's Supreme Court, which heard the case in 1824.

In its early years, the Supreme Court's proceedings were relaxed, even languorous. Today, oral arguments in the Court are short, frequently interrupted by the justices, and often cut off in mid-sentence. In the early 1800s, the Court had little business, so lawyers were allowed to present their cases for hours, sometimes days. This invitation to extended advocacy in momentous cases attracted the top lawyers of the day, men with storied or exotic names like William Pinckney, William Wirt, Luther Martin, Reverdy Johnson and, most especially, Daniel Webster.

New Hampshire congressman, Massachusetts senator, secretary of state, fervent champion of and spokesman for a Union frayed for decades by sectional discord, Webster, the God-like Daniel, is one of America's greatest statesmen. The best orator of his age, rivaled only by Henry Clay, school children for generations memorized his Second Reply to Hayne during the sectional crisis of 1830, pleading for "liberty *and* union, now and forever, one and inseparable," and his Seventh of March Speech, telling his Senate colleagues as he rose to support the Compromise of 1850 that "I speak today for the preservation of the Union. Hear me for my cause."

Engaged as he was as senator and statesman, Webster was not a full time legislator. Like the Supreme Court, the United States Senate in its early years had little business and short, infrequent sessions. Senators had time to do other things, and they were unfettered by modern-day rules and ethical standards limiting outside pursuits. In this accommodating environment, Webster used his oratorical powers and legal skills to establish a flourishing Supreme Court practice. He became and remains one of the Court's most skillful advocates, representing the winning side in a number of Marshall court cases, including *McCulloch v. Maryland* and the Dartmouth College case. In *Gibbons v. Ogden*,[19] as counsel for Gibbons, he challenged the New York monopoly.

John Marshall was a Federalist, temperamentally disposed to promote a national economy and to support a robust exercise of federal power. With Marshall on the bench and Webster at the bar, poor Ogden didn't have a chance. In his opinion Marshall quickly concluded that Congress' exercise of its interstate commerce powers in the coastal trading act trumped the attempt by New York to control use of its waters, giving Gibbons as holder of a trading act license the right to use the New York waters despite the Fulton-Livingston monopoly. Marshall could have stopped there, but he liked to paint in broad strokes, and he proceeded to do just that.

In words that would echo down the years, Marshall said that the power of Congress over interstate commerce is "complete in itself, may be exercised to its utmost extent, and acknowledges no limitations other than as are prescribed in the Constitution." Then, in a brilliant rhetorical and analytical display, he used fear of state obstructions to suggest that Congress' power to control interstate commerce was a preemptive power, completely excluding any power in the states even if Congress had not acted. Recognizing, however, that states might incidentally regulate interstate commerce in the exercise of other powers, he indicated that this incidental regulation of interstate commerce was acceptable unless Congress prohibited it.

Gibbons v. Ogden established the framework for dividing state from federal power in the regulation of interstate commerce. Accepting Marshall's conclusion that the states cannot disrupt interstate commerce, the Supreme Court, through a principle quaintly called the "Dormant Commerce Clause," holds that the states cannot "unduly burden" interstate commerce even if Congress has not acted. If state action incidentally burdens commerce, the burden is permitted unless Congress decides otherwise.

Gibbons v. Ogden does not directly address regulation of private conduct under the interstate commerce clause, but it has consistently been used and misused for that purpose.

We are, however, getting ahead of the story, for *Gibbons* was far-reaching but slow-acting, delayed first by a lack of interstate commerce and then by a conservative Supreme Court.

The Conservative Interlude

In 1824 the United States had a rural, horse and wagon economy, with only a smattering of local commerce and industry. The Erie Canal, linking New York City to the Great Lakes, was a year away, and five years would pass before Charles Carroll of Carrolton, the last living signer of the Declaration of Independence, dedicated the Baltimore and Ohio railroad, inaugurating an age of rails that would transform the economy but was slow to develop. There was no telegraph or other means of rapid communication, limited and rudimentary use of the nation's waterways, and few roads. Things would stay this way for decades to come. With little interstate commerce, there was little need to employ the interstate commerce clause.

And then, as Lincoln said, the war came. Between 1861 and 1865, the North developed its mines and industries, marshaled its forces and resources, and deployed them against the South, ultimately prevailing with overwhelming manpower and materials and the aggressive, Confederacy-constricting strategy of Generals Grant, Sherman and Sheridan. The war primed the economy for post-war expansion, and Congress encouraged development with a national banking law, a homestead act and legislation to establish a transcontinental railroad.

In the post-war decades, the economy sired by the war and its enabling legislation thrived and expanded. On May 10, 1869, in Promontory Point, Utah, the last spike was driven in the first transcontinental railroad. By the end of the century railroads stitched the country together. Immigrants arrived by the boatload, settling mostly in urban areas already swelling from a native influx drawn by a growing economy, while other people moved west. Nebraska joined the Union in 1867, Colorado in 1876, the Dakotas, Montana and Washington in 1889, and Wyoming and Idaho in 1890, the year in which the Census Bureau said that the American frontier had passed from land to lore. (Utah did not join the fraternity until 1896, after it had banned plural marriages.)

Industries developed and became national by using railroads and waterways to gather raw materials and distribute products and targeting the expanding, increasingly urbanized population as employees and customers. Competition was fierce, ruthless, sometimes unfair. Only the strongest survived. Employing "trusts"—legal devices for combining and controlling competitive ventures—and other anti-competitive tactics, John D. Rockefeller and his partners dominated oil, Andrew Carnegie and Henry Clay Frick coke and steel, Rockefeller and Carnegie iron, Edward Harriman and James J. Hill railroads, Henry Havemeyer sugar, Phillip Armour meat packing. In 1901 J.P. Morgan cornered Carnegie on a golf course and convinced him to combine with his competitors, creating United States Steel, the largest industrial corporation in the world.

With progress came problems. The trusts absorbed or destroyed competitors. Railroads gouged small shippers and favored large ones with rebates and other preferences. Meat packers sold adulterated food. And they all oppressed their workers, driving down wages, employing children, demanding long days and full weeks, neglecting safety measures and firing those who promoted or joined a union.

In response to these abuses, Congress exerted its powers under the interstate commerce clause. In 1887 it enacted the Interstate Commerce Act, providing for the regulation of railroads, followed in 1890 by the Sherman Antitrust Act, in 1906 by the Food and Drug Act (prompted by Upton Sinclair's graphic description of the meat packing industry in *The Jungle*), and later by laws controlling wages and hours, child labor and conditions in the coal industry.

When these laws were challenged in the Supreme Court, the Court gave them a mixed but generally hostile reception. It upheld the Interstate Commerce and Food and Drug acts,[20] and it allowed use of the Sherman Antitrust Act to dismantle the Hill-Harriman combine and Rockefeller's Standard Oil empire.[21] (In a perverse twist, the Standard Oil divestiture enriched Rockefeller as the aggregate value of the parts soon exceeded the value of the prior whole, making Rockefeller a billionaire at a time when America's annual gross domestic product was $35 billion. For Bill Gates to have the same relation to today's GDP, he would need about $340 billion.) On the other hand, it struck down the wage and hour and child labor laws on the grounds that they protected employees in manufacturing and mining, which it distinguished from commerce.[22] For the same reason, the Court said that the

Sherman Antitrust Act could not be used to keep Havemeyer's American Sugar Refining Company from acquiring four additional manufacturing facilities.[23] Justice Holmes authored an opinion holding that major league baseball was not interstate commerce.[24] As we will see in Chapter 3, the Court's hostility to federal economic legislation from the 1890s through the 1930s was matched during these years by its use of the Fourteenth Amendment's due process clause to strike down state attempts to protect workers and respond to corporate power.

And then, in the late 1930s, suddenly, abruptly, permanently, the Court changed, influenced by the economic and political consequences of the Great Depression and intimidated by President Franklin Roosevelt's threat to pack the Court by expanding its membership from nine to 15. After 1937 the Court never again used the due process clause to invalidate state economic legislation, and it moved quickly and decisively to uphold congressional exercise of the interstate commerce clause.

The first straw in the wind was a 1937 decision rejecting Jones & Laughlin Steel's contention that its manufacturing facilities could not be subjected to the National Labor Relations Act, which protected union organizing activities and established labor standards.[25] Its manufacturing facilities, the Court said, were a part of Jones & Laughlin's interstate operations, and could be regulated as such.

The Jones and Laughlin decision departs from the earlier decisions primarily in tone, but *United States v. Darby*, decided four years later, rejected the earlier approach, upholding a federal law that banned interstate shipment of manufactured goods made by employees who made less than the minimum wage established by the Fair Labor Standards Act.[26] Citing Marshall's *Gibbons v. Ogden* dictum that congressional power over interstate commerce was "plenary and complete in itself" and "could be exercised to its utmost extent," the Court said that the shipment ban was a legitimate exercise of this plenary regulatory power.

Darby was just a warm up for the dam breaker. A year later Justice Robert Jackson got the case of farmer Filburn and his 11 acre wheat allotment.

Feeling His Wheat

Robert Houghwout Jackson is the last of a dead breed, a Supreme Court justice who didn't go to college or graduate from law school. Admitted to the bar in 1913, he established a flourishing practice in upstate New York and became a friend, political supporter and poker playing intimate of Franklin Roosevelt. Roosevelt brought him to Washington in 1934 as a lawyer for the IRS, elevated him to solicitor general and attorney general, and in 1941 appointed him to the Supreme Court. There, in a career interrupted by service as chief prosecutor at the Nuremberg trials and cut short by early death, he became one of the Court's near-great justices.[27] Less cryptic than Holmes, less cerebral and ethereal than Justice Benjamin Cardozo, Jackson was the best stylist ever to sit on the Court. In the years to come he would team with Justice Felix Frankfurter to exert a moderate and even conservative restraint on the liberal firebrands on the Roosevelt Court, but in 1942 he was fresh from the rolls as chief defender of the Roosevelt economic program, and in *Wickard v. Filburn*[28] he proved his mettle.

Under the Agricultural Adjustment Act of 1938, the Secretary of Agriculture set quotas for wheat production in an attempt to control its price. Filburn was a dairy farmer who grew wheat for use in his dairy operation. The Secretary subjected Filburn to the act even though he sold no wheat, and established his 1941 quota at about 11 acres. He exceeded his quota by a few acres and was fined $117. He contested his fine, and his case made it to the Supreme Court.

Jackson was determined to uphold the fine, but he had two problems. Filburn didn't sell any wheat, either locally or in the national market, so his wheat production and consumption was not commerce for purpose of a program regulating commerce in wheat. And if his operation had been commerce, it was obviously too small by itself to affect interstate commerce.

These problems didn't stop Jackson, or even slow him down. Quoting Marshall's expansive statement of congressional power under the interstate commerce clause, Jackson said that Congress could regulate any activity, local or non-local, commercial or non-commercial, if it exerted a substantial effect on interstate commerce. And, he said, for purposes of determining whether Filburn exerted a substantial effect on interstate commerce, you could lump him in with other farmers and consider their aggregate impact.

What Justice Jackson cooked up from 11 acres of wheat was unbounded federal power. After *Wickard*, nearly everything could be justified in the name of the interstate commerce clause. As the owner of Ollie's Barbecue in Birmingham, Alabama, could assure you, nearly everything has been.

When Judge Sarah Hughes administered the presidential oath to Lyndon Johnson a few hours after John F. Kennedy's assassination, presidential power passed to a man with political skills matched only by Lincoln and Franklin Roosevelt. The Johnson who emerges from Robert Caro's breathtaking multi-volume biography was a genius in the art of amassing and exercising power. In 1964, buoyed by a widespread public desire to enact Kennedy's unfinished agenda, exerting presidential power in ways both honorable and devious, buttonholing, arm-twisting, cajoling, pleading, log-rolling, threatening and intimidating as only Lyndon Johnson could, Johnson did what no modern president had been able to do—he defeated a Southern filibuster en route to passage of the first comprehensive civil rights law of the 20th century.

The Civil Rights Act of 1964 prohibits discrimination on the basis of race, color, religion or national origin in public accommodations, gas stations, restaurants and theaters and other places of exhibition or entertainment. The act is based on the interstate commerce clause, so facilities are subject to the act only if they are "in commerce," but this is broadly defined to include all transient lodging facilities, whether or not they serve interstate travelers, all gas stations and restaurants that serve interstate travelers or buy any substantial part of their inventory in interstate commerce, and all theaters and other places of exhibition or entertainment that regularly present films, performers, sporting events or other sources of entertainment that have moved in interstate commerce.

The transient guest provisions of the act were upheld by the Supreme Court in a case involving the Heart of Atlanta Motel, a 216 room motel in downtown Atlanta.[29] The motel did cater to interstate travelers, but the Court held that Congress could apply the law to all transient lodging facilities, regardless of the source of their customers. On the same day, the Court held that the act could be applied to Ollie's Barbecue.

Ollie's Barbecue was a 220 seat restaurant in Birmingham, Alabama. Eleven blocks from the nearest interstate highway, farther than that from any railroad or bus stations, it served only local customers and bought all of its food from local suppliers. One of those suppliers, however, purchased its stock from another state, and that was enough, said the Court, to subject Ollie's to the act. Relying heavily on *Wickard*, the Court said that Congress could regulate restaurants serving only local customers based on evidence that racially segregated restaurants depressed interstate travel by Blacks and discouraged Blacks from moving to the area.[30]

Congressional use of the interstate commerce clause to combat discrimination did not end with the Civil Rights Act of 1964. In the Fair Housing Act of 1968, Congress prohibited discrimination on the basis of race, color, religion, sex, or familial or handicapped status in the sale, rental or financing of housing. The act applies to the rental of any facility containing four or more units, to any property owner who sells or leases three or more homes or rental units in a year, and to any agent who sells or leases two or more homes or rental units in a year. The Americans With Disabilities Act of 1990 mandates handicap accessibility standards for nearly all buildings. Both of these statutes regulate activities only remotely related to interstate commerce, but both have been upheld by the courts.

Our response to the civil rights cases is colored by our support for the outcome. The civil rights acts of the '60s expressed a belated response to the inhumanity of slavery and the injustice of racial discrimination, and they have transformed America's society and lifted its economy—a boon to North and South alike. Nobody expects and few hope that the Supreme Court will overrule these cases. Still, the question remains whether these acts can pass constitutional muster under the interstate commerce clause. To consider this question, it helps to slightly change the facts in a way that extracts emotion from analysis.

Let's assume that, in the years before passage of the federal civil rights laws, several Northern states enact state anti-discrimination and accessibility laws similar to those later enacted by Congress. Controlled by Southern and Northern conservatives, Congress finds that these laws deter Southern Whites from traveling to or moving north and that the handicapped accessibility laws prompt builders to favor states that don't have the laws, and voids the laws—preempts them, in the lingo of constitutional law. The states sue, claiming that the laws' limited effect on interstate commerce does not justify federal preemption. The case comes to the Supreme Court. Who wins? If you said Congress, my guess is better than yours. Clearly, in the federal civil rights laws social engineering is masquerading as commercial regulation.

Wickard does insist that Congress can regulate private activity or conduct only if it has a "substantial" effect on interstate commerce, and this requirement is echoed in two recent Supreme Court cases holding that the interstate commerce clause could not justify prosecution under the Gun-Free School Zone Act or the Violence Against Women Act.[31] This requirement is not a meaningful limitation, however, both because "substantial" is in the eye of the beholder and because the impact need not be on interstate commerce as a whole, but only on an identifiable market, category or segment of commerce. In *Wickard*, the interstate wheat market was a small part of the national economy, and in the cases upholding the civil rights acts, the affected markets—those who change their residence from one state to another, for example—are often small and even inconsequential segments of interstate commerce. When it comes to affected market segments, any little fish in the big interstate commerce pond will do, as shown in the cases of the red-coated wolf[32] and the long-name fly.[33]

On his North Carolina farm, Richard Lee Mann kept a wary watch on the red wolves menacing his cattle, and he shot one he thought was about to attack. Hauled into court under the Endangered Species Act, Mann said he couldn't see how his non-commercial killing of a wild animal on his own land affected interstate commerce. You didn't look hard enough, the Fourth Circuit Court of Appeals replied in holding that he had violated the act. The wolf's death, the court said, affected the interstate travel of those who wanted to see the wolf or hear it at "howling events" held in North Carolina, as well as the possible future market in the red wolves' pelts once their endangered species days were over. The court said that the "national wildlife industry" brought in about $29 billion per year—about one fourth of one percent of the national economy—but it didn't quantify the endangered species share of that industry or the annual take from the interstate travel of wild animal enthusiasts. We do know that the possible future market in red wolf pelts is zero percent of interstate commerce. Whatever the facts are, we are obviously dealing with extremely small segments of interstate commerce. The Supreme Court refused to take an appeal from the Fourth Circuit's decision.

The Delhi Sands Flower-Loving Fly lives only in a very small part of California. The fly was placed on the endangered species list. The federal Fish and Wildlife Service told San Bernardino County that construction of a hospital would violate the Endangered Species Act because a traffic interchange needed to service the hospital would endanger the fly's habitat. The National Association of Homebuilders and others appealed the FWS decision, claiming that the interstate commerce clause could not be used to protect the habitat of this very localized creature. The appellants lost their appeal in the United States Court of Appeals for the District of Columbia. In a long opinion and with a straight face, the court said that the elimination of endangered species would have a "staggering" effect on "bio-diversity," and thus on the "current and future commerce that relies on a diverse array of species." It didn't say what the annual revenues from this commerce was, but it seems clear that neither the commerce based upon a "diverse array of species" nor the endangered species share of that commerce is a significant slice of interstate commerce. Again, the Supreme Court refused an appeal.

Bad as these decisions are, others are even worse, with an even more tenuous connection between interstate commerce and the regulated conduct. For example, the courts have used the interstate commerce clause to justify blanket congressional control over migratory birds, whether or not any commercial activity is involved,[34] and to permit criminal prosecution for possession of a gun that hadn't moved in interstate commerce for decades,[35] arson involving a two unit apartment building,[36] a racial attack in a local park,[37] and possession of animal parts that had never moved in commerce.[38]

The outcomes under these interstate commerce clause cases would be bad enough if they always reflected the considered will of Congress. In many cases, however, the excesses result from the actions of over-zealous prosecutors and bureaucrats and environmentalists exercising a privileged status.

As a general rule, a person gains access to court or non-public administrative proceedings only if he has a dog in the fight—a personal interest or position that will benefit or suffer from the outcome. And it must be a big dog. All taxpayers are affected by expenditures of public monies, but the courts have consistently held that taxpayers cannot go to court just because they don't like the way their tax dollars are working.

This is the general rule, but it is often relaxed for environmental groups. Many state and federal laws admit them to courtrooms and administrative chambers even though they have no personal stake in the outcome. They can pressure administrators for an expansive or even imaginative application of, say, the Endangered Species Act, and go to court if they don't get their way. Private rights and property are thus placed at risk, not by congressional will, but by bureaucrats and judges yielding to special interest groups.

No matter how you look at it or where you look at it from, the picture of the interstate commerce clause that emerges from the cases referred to above (and many others like them) is deeply troubling.

The outcome in these cases cannot be squared with the structure of the government established by the Constitution. It is a government of limited powers, not the government of nearly unlimited reach created since 1937 by a grasping Congress, an empire-building bureaucracy, an agenda-pushing gaggle of special interest groups and a cooperative judiciary.

The decisions are at odds with the purpose of the commerce clause, which is a practical provision crafted by experienced men, designed to promote and protect a national economy, not to serve as an open-ended source and justification of federal power. They are also at odds with the words of the commerce clause, which applies to interstate commerce, not to activity that either has nothing to do with interstate commerce or can be linked to it only by a leap of faith or imagination.

The structure, purpose and words of the Constitution are thus all arrayed against the courts' construction of the interstate commerce clause. Reflection on what was *not* in the Constitution when it was adopted is just as instructive.

When the Constitution was drafted, adopted and ratified, there was no Bill of Rights. A Bill of Rights had been discussed during the ratification process, but it was not assured, and in any event no one proposed or ratified the interstate commerce clause with the understanding that it had a reach that would be narrowed by a future Bill of Rights. We must therefore consider the courts' version of the commerce clause on the assumption that there is no Bill of Rights. Their version could be used to devastate the liberties protected by the Bill of Rights.

Wickard v. Filburn allows the regulation of non-commercial activities that have a substantial impact on interstate commerce when lumped with similar activities by others. The wheat control program that nailed farmer Filburn was only one program under the Agricultural Adjustment Act. The entire act had a greater impact on interstate commerce than the wheat program, and its impact of course depended on whether it was enacted or defeated. Those who supported or opposed the act, whether by lobbying or petitioning Congress, assembling or speaking for or against it, expressing editorial support or opposition, or other activities, had a far greater impact on interstate commerce than Filburn did. In the absence of a Bill of Rights, Congress could on the *Wickard* rationale prohibit or restrict all of these non-commercial activities. The impact does not stop with passage of the act. Administrators decide how the act is to be applied, so Congress could prohibit or restrict activities calculated to influence their decisions. In the absence of a Bill of Rights, Congress could also use *Wickard* to outlaw trade boycotts and demonstrations that diminished interstate commerce.

The doctrine of the *Darby* case, allowing Congress to exclude safe, legal, non-harmful products from interstate commerce, would be even more destructive than *Wickard* in a world without a Bill of Rights. Nearly all commercial and non-commercial communication and expression—every newspaper, magazine, book, internet blog—use interstate commerce. Without a Bill of Rights, Congress could under the *Darby* doctrine prohibit or regulate all content it considered dangerous, immoral, injurious, incendiary, "fraught with death," in Justice Holmes' expressive term, or otherwise improper.

Cutting Samson's Hair

Given steroids by Congress and the courts, the interstate commerce clause has bulked-up to unconstitutional, samsonian strength. How do we cut this Samson's hair, shearing enough to eliminate his ill-gotten power without depriving him of the strength necessary to do his job?

Returning to the pre-1937 cases distinguishing production from commerce would not be practical or helpful. The cases attempt to draw a distinction that is hard to draw and is not realistic in an integrated industrial economy. In any event, Congress these days is not regulating production, but everything else.

The attempt to restrict the commerce clause by insisting that the regulated activities have a "substantial" impact is not promising, both because "substantial" is in the eye of the beholder and because, as we have seen, courts can always find a significant impact on some sliver of commerce or, as in the red wolf case, some possible future commerce. The Supreme Court's refusal to hear the Endangered Species appeals suggests that it does not propose to use "substantial" to work a significant change in the law, and the Court confirmed this in its June 2005 decision allowing use of the commerce clause to regulate back yard marijuana patches. Other approaches that have been suggested as a basis for restraining the commerce power, such as distinguishing between "direct" and "indirect" effects on interstate commerce, have also come a cropper.

The source of the explosive growth of the commerce power under the post-1937 cases is the use of "regulate" in the provision empowering Congress to "regulate commerce among the several states."

The common meaning of "regulate" is "to control or direct according to principle, rule or law." *American Heritage Dictionary* (4th Ed. 2000). It is clear from the cases, including dictum in *Gibbons v. Ogden*, that this is the definition the courts use to apply the interstate commerce clause. It is a power-conferring, command and control definition that seemingly gives Congress unfettered regulatory power over interstate commerce in all respects and at all points, no matter how insignificant the regulation might be to the protection or functioning of interstate commerce as a whole. This power to regulate any detail also makes it easy to expand and extend congressional power, for as we have seen in the small fish in a big pond cases, it allows Congress to demand a power to regulate anything that affects its ability to control that detail. Congress, abetted by the courts, has mounted "regulate" and ridden it to hell.

But if "regulate" is the problem in the unwarranted exercise of federal power under the commerce clause, it also provides the solution, for Congress and the courts have been using the wrong definition of "regulate."

To state again the common meaning of "regulate," it is the power "to control or direct according to rule, principle or law."

The first part of this definition, identifying a power to prescribe, prohibit or restrict, does not square with the purpose of the interstate commerce clause. As we have seen, Congress was empowered to regulate interstate commerce because the states had obstructed that commerce. The purpose of the clause is to liberate commerce, not control or restrict it. When Marshall admitted New Jersey boats to New York waters, he regulated commerce in a manner contemplated by the Constitution. When Grant's army forced the surrender of Vicksburg, freeing commerce on the Mississippi River and prompting Lincoln to exult that "the Father of Waters again goes unvexed to the sea," it regulated commerce as contemplated by the Constitution.

The second part of the definition, requiring that the regulation be "according to rule, principle or law," also fails to describe "regulate" as used in the interstate commerce clause. Implicit in "according to" is a need for a stated standard or framework to guide the regulation. This part of the common meaning is well known, reflected in the thousands of pages of administrative regulations issued to implement federal statutes. It was clearly known to the Founders, for Article I, Section 8 of the Constitution gives Congress the power "to make *rules* for the *regulation* of the land and naval forces." (Emphasis added.) The Constitution sets forth no standard or framework to guide regulation under the interstate commerce clause.

There is another definition of "regulate" that can be used to describe government power. The last definition of "regulate" in *American Heritage Dictionary* is "to put or maintain in order."

This definition fits the use of "regulate" in the commerce clause, and, unlike the command and control definition, it lends itself readily to the fact that the commerce power is a limited power. It recognizes that interstate commerce was disorderly—hamstrung by the states—when the Constitution was adopted and empowers Congress on an ongoing basis to promote and protect commerce. It shifts the focus of the clause from regulation of commerce to the commerce itself, considered as a whole, making it difficult to use "regulate" as an open-ended invitation to exercise federal power. The question is whether there is evidence that the Constitution does use this definition of "regulate" in the commerce clause.

There is indeed. Unlike the command and control definition of "regulate," the orderly commerce definition is responsive to the history and purpose of the Constitution, well-suited to achieve its goal of liberating, promoting and protecting commerce. The shoe fits. In addition to this history and purpose evidence, there is substantial indication in the words of the Constitution that "regulate" is used in an orderly commerce sense.

Congressional powers are listed in Article 1, Section 8 of the Constitution. In an entry four lines below the commerce clause, Congress is empowered "to coin money and regulate the value thereof and of federal coin." The value of money is not susceptible to command, so "regulate" in this provision contemplates action to stabilize the currency—to put and maintain it in order. The value of money could, for example, be maintained by increasing or decreasing its supply. The Founders were thus clearly aware of, and used, "regulate" in the sense of to put and maintain in order. They also knew and used "regulate" in its common, command and control sense, for later in Section 8 they empower Congress to "make rules for the government and regulation of the land and naval forces." In the commerce clause "regulate" is set forth as it is in the nearby coinage provision, as a stand-alone, unadorned verb, much different from the use of "regulation" in the armed services provision. As he crafted the Constitution, what is the likelihood that Gouverneur Morris used "regulate" in the same way but with different meanings in the space of 40 words?

In the Constitution and nearly-contemporaneous Bill of Rights there are only three uses of "regulate" as a verb—the commerce clause, the coinage clause, and the now-controversial Second Amendment, which states that "a well-regulated militia, being necessary to the security of a free state, the right of the people to keep and bear arms shall not be infringed." Here, "well-regulated" does not mean subjected to regulations, but rather orderly, well-drilled. The Second Amendment provides further evidence that the Founders were aware of the "put and maintain in order" meaning of "regulate," and further evidence that it has this meaning in the commerce clause, for a rule of statutory construction assumes that a word has the same meaning throughout a document.

There is evidence in the commerce clause itself that "regulate" is used in an orderly commerce sense. The clause empowers Congress "to regulate commerce with foreign nations, and among the several states, and with the Indian tribes." (When the Constitution was adopted, Indian tribes not yet absorbed into American society were largely located outside the boundaries of the United States.) There is a principle of statutory construction that words of a feather flock together—that associated words or provisions have the same general meaning. Under this principle, "regulate" means the same for interstate, foreign and tribal commerce. Foreign and tribal commerce cannot be regulated by Congress in a command and control sense, for most of it occurs outside the United States, and one party to the commerce—the foreign nation or the tribe—is not subject to the jurisdiction of the

United States. The only meaning of "regulate" that works here is a power to develop and protect an orderly commerce. As with the regulation of interstate commerce, this use of "regulate" is consistent with the history and purpose of the foreign commerce clause, for in the years before the Constitution was adopted the states obstructed foreign as well as interstate commerce.

Assuming that "regulate" in the interstate commerce clause means "to put or maintain in order," what are the implications? More specifically, how does this meaning deliver a practical, workable restriction of congressional power to regulate private conduct under the commerce clause while recognizing the legitimate scope of that power? How, in short, does it cut Samson's hair?

The orderly commerce clause focuses on interstate commerce as a whole and returns the interstate commerce clause to its role as protector and promoter of interstate commerce, designed primarily to thwart state attempts to obstruct or disrupt commerce. This is certainly Marshall's vision of the commerce clause in *Gibbons v. Ogden* as he announces what comes to be known as the dormant commerce clause, designed to keep the states at bay. With the new meaning and the old background in mind, I believe there are three categories in which Congress can regulate private conduct under the interstate commerce clause.

1. *Protection of the channels of interstate commerce.* Congress can prevent and outlaw attacks on and threats to interstate commerce. Under this heading would be laws criminalizing train robberies, terrorist attacks, creation of internet viruses and the like. Commerce may not be orderly if it cannot be protected.

2. Dormant commerce clause. The second category of permissible federal regulation of private conduct under an orderly commerce approach is conduct that the states can't regulate because of the dormant commerce clause. The dormant commerce clause is the doctrine that identifies an area in which the states can't act even if Congress hasn't prohibited them from doing so. For example, the states can't regulate the rates charged for the interstate transport of goods or people by railroads, airlines, trucks or other common carriers even if Congress has not established these rates, so Congress could regulate these rates if it wanted to. This second category of congressional power recognizes the core function of the interstate commerce clause and avoids a power vacuum, allowing Congress to walk where the states cannot tread.

3. Preemption area. The third category of permissible congressional regulation of private conduct under an orderly commerce approach is the power to regulate conduct if, and only if, Congress could preempt state laws regulating that conduct, regardless of whether or not it has chosen to do so. Under the commerce clause explored by Marshall in *Gibbons v Ogden* and subsequently applied by the Supreme Court, Congress can preempt state regulations or actions that could disrupt or obstruct interstate commerce. Examples include state laws regulating wages and hours, labor standards and securities and financial transactions, and other state laws, such as California's stringent pollution control laws and laws restricting the length and weight of semis, that could disrupt or burden interstate commerce if commerce and industry are forced to comply with different laws in different states. Under this category of permitted congressional action, Congress could control private conduct in these areas. Tying congressional power over private conduct to its preemption power over the states recognizes that the primary mission of the commerce clause is to shield commerce from disruptive state action and to promote a national economy, not to regulate conduct that the states can regulate. It embraces the concept of an orderly interstate commerce considered as a whole, for the preemption power by its very nature focuses on private conduct that has a widespread impact on the national economy—Congress could not preempt state laws that have limited impact on interstate commerce. It rejects the command and control approach, barring nit-picking regulations and far-fetched constructions. It responds to the spirit of the Tenth Amendment, keeping the feds from the states' turf.

Descending to specifics, the catalog of congressional powers listed above would allow regulation of activities with a national or widespread impact, as suggested by the examples in category 3, but would not allow regulation of activities having little or no impact on interstate commerce. The catalog would allow Congress to prohibit discrimination in employment, maybe in transient lodging, but not otherwise. The catalog would force Congress out of most land use regulation, depriving it of power to restrict development or land use under the Endangered Species Act, Wild Rivers Act, laws extending federal jurisdiction to wetlands having little or no impact on interstate or navigable wetlands, or other laws restricting local development or land use under color of the interstate commerce clause, for Congress could almost certainly not preempt state laws in these areas, and it has never attempted to do so. It would not allow Congress to exclude safe, legal products from interstate commerce or to criminalize conduct having little or no affect on interstate commerce.

The catalog would in most cases not allow the regulation of non-commercial activity. Congress could not control wheat or marijuana grown for the grower's own use. If Richard Lee Mann drew a bead on marauding wolves, he might want to know where the state game warden was, but he wouldn't have to worry about the federales. The long-name fly would have to look for local protectors. An owner who torched a two-unit apartment building would be caught and punished by local authorities.

Most importantly, the catalog would stand watch against future attempts by Congress, the bureaucrats and special interest groups to improperly use the interstate commerce clause to expand their power, build their empires or advance their agendas.

CHAPTER 3

The Due Process Clause —
Legislators in Robes

Liberals had a problem. The United States Supreme Court had already misused the due process clause of the Fourteenth Amendment to give them most of what they needed to secure their social and cultural agenda, but it wasn't quite enough. What they needed, and hadn't yet got, was a doctrine that created a constitutional right to an abortion on demand for the first six months of pregnancy without giving any aid or comfort to property rights. That gave a fully quickened fetus less protection than a long-name fly or a snail darter. That, in short, allowed liberals to have their cake and edicts too. And to get it, they had to overcome Supreme Court decisions hostile to claimed rights not included in any specific provisions of the Constitution.

They got it. Not from state legislators. Not from Congress. They got it from the United States Supreme Court that had already enacted most of their agenda. The story of the Court's enactment of this agenda, capped by its passage of a right to abortion on demand, is a 100 year drama starring a Supreme Court quartet called substantive due process, Footnote Four, the incorporation doctrine and the right to privacy. It is a story in which turnabout becomes foul play. Conservatives invented substantive due process and used it to protect property rights for about 60 years. Starting in the late 1930s, liberals seized substantive due process, applied it in a way that stripped property of most of its protection, and used it as the foundation for the liberal-serving concepts of Footnote Four, the incorporation doctrine and the right to privacy. When the curtain fell, liberal judicial legislation stood triumphant and alone at center stage.

We will follow this drama as it unfolds.

Substantive Due Process—Off on the Wrong Track

The Fourteenth Amendment of the Constitution, adopted in 1868, provides that "no state shall make or enforce any law which shall abridge the privileges or immunities of citizens of the United States; nor shall any state deprive any person of life, liberty, or property, without due process of law." These clauses are called the privileges and immunities clause and the due process clause. This chapter deals with the due process clause.

With its use of "process," the due process clause seems to envision procedural safeguards—notice and opportunity to be heard, right to counsel and to confront witnesses, right to jury trial, limits on investigation techniques and means of collecting evidence, and the like. If Justice Samuel Miller had had his way, the due process clause probably would have been limited to procedural safeguards.

Born in Kentucky, trained as a doctor, self-taught as a lawyer, Miller moved to Iowa because of his opposition to slavery. An early and active member of the Iowa Republican Party, he supported Lincoln in 1860 and was rewarded by appointment to the Supreme Court in 1862. In a 28 year career punctuated by service on the commission appointed to pick the winner of the contested 1876 presidential election, Miller forged a reputation as one of the Court's near-great justices. In 1873, he spoke for the Court in the case of the displaced butchers.

Appalled by the sordid conditions in the New Orleans slaughterhouses, concerned about an expected flood of Texas cattle, and convinced that a single operator would address the problems posed by a multitude of small, hard-to-police slaughterhouses, the Louisiana legislature gave Crescent City Livestock Landing and Slaughter-House Company a 25 year monopoly on landing and slaughtering livestock in New Orleans. Several displaced butchers challenged this monopoly in the Louisiana courts, lost in the Louisiana Supreme Court and appealed to the United States Supreme Court. The Court combined the proceedings into a single appeal known to history as the *Slaughter-House Cases*.[39]

The butchers claimed that the monopoly deprived them of their right to pursue their trade in violation of the privileges and immunities and due process clauses. Miller gave them short shrift. Asserting that the Fourteenth Amendment was adopted primarily for the benefit of ex-slaves, he held that neither of these clauses protected a right to pursue a vocation. While he rejected the butchers' claims under both clauses, he focused on the privileges and immunities clause, limiting its reach to a few narrowly-defined, pre-existing rights that did not include a right to pursue a vocation.

Justices Stephen Field and Joseph Bradley, both of whom would join Miller on the 1876 presidential electoral commission, dissented in separate opinions. Field found a right to pursue a vocation in the privileges and immunities clause.

Bradley agreed, but then suggested that the due process clause also protected this right, contending that a right to pursue a vocation was both a "liberty" and a "property" protected by the due process clause.

After the *Slaughter-House Cases*, the privileges and immunities clause was pretty much a dead letter. Miller's cramped reading of the clause reduced it to an insignificance from which it has never recovered.

On the other hand, Justice Bradley's vision of the due process clause was alive if not well. Bradley understood that the due process clause required states to adopt fair procedures, but he also believed that the clause limited the states' power to impair liberty and regulate property. The use of the due process clause as a limit on state power has come to be called "substantive due process," while its use to require procedural safeguards is called "procedural due process." Simply stated, substantive due process limits what states can do, while procedural due process regulates the procedures by which they do it. Miller refused to adopt substantive due process to support the butchers' case, but he didn't consider whether it might be used to give protection to liberty or property rights in other circumstances.

Field looked for other circumstances. A Connecticut Yankee, Field moved to California during the Gold Rush days, won election to the California Supreme Court, where he survived an assassination attempt by a fellow justice (Field's bodyguard killed the other judge), and was appointed by Lincoln to the Supreme Court in 1863. In a 34 year career he was a fierce defender of property rights, urging use of the Fourteenth Amendment to fend off economic regulation. His first post-*Slaughter House* effort came in *Munn v. Illinois*, one of the so-called Granger Cases.[40]

Locked in unequal battle with those who stored and moved their products, Midwestern farmers in the 1860s banded together in groups called Granges. Politically potent in states still largely rural, these groups lobbied to regulate railroads and storage facilities. In 1871 Illinois responded to this pressure by enacting a law regulating rates for grain-storage warehouses. The warehouse operators challenged the law, lost in the state courts, and appealed to the Supreme Court in 1877.

The Grangers won. Stating that railroads and storage facilities were "affected with a public interest," and referring to a well-established body of law permitting regulation of ventures so affected, the Court held that the state could regulate the warehouse rates.

Field dissented vigorously. Sensing that Miller had killed the privileges and immunities clause, Field adopted Bradley's *Slaughter-House* approach. The rate regulations, he said, deprived the warehouse owners of property rights and economic liberties in violation of substantive due process.

Nine years later, in the *Railroad Commission Cases*, the Supreme Court adopted substantive due process as the basis for its decision.[41] Minnesota's railroad regulators imposed rates that gave the railroads an unreasonably low rate of return, and the Minnesota Supreme Court said it had no authority to increase or reject the rates. The United States Supreme Court did what the Minnesota court had refused to do, holding that unreasonably low rates deprived railroads of their property in violation of substantive due process. Field had won.

With the Minnesota case, the Supreme Court accepted substantive due process, but its reach was limited. It was easy to conclude that the states could not impose confiscatory rates of return. The Court had not yet used substantive due process as a general restraint on economic legislation.

That came in 1897, in *Allgeyer v. Louisiana*, in an opinion written by Justice Rufus Peckham of New York, just before

Field reluctantly retired (he had to be talked off the Court.)[42] Finding freedom of contract in the due process clause, Peckham held that Louisiana could not prevent its citizens from buying insurance from out-of-state insurers not licensed in Louisiana. Substantive due process, he said, includes the right of a citizen "to be free in the enjoyment of all his faculties; to be free to use them in all lawful ways; to live and work where he will; to earn his livelihood in any lawful calling; to pursue any livelihood or avocation; and to enter into all contracts" needed to achieve these purposes.

Peckham struck again in 1905, in a case that gave its name to the era in which the Supreme Court used substantive due process to nullify state legislation regulating economic activities. *Lochner v. New York* voided a law limiting the hours that bakers could work, holding that the law impaired the bakers' freedom to contract for whatever hours they wanted.[43] Justice Holmes wrote a stinging dissent, asserting that "a constitution is not intended to embody a particular economic theory, whether of paternalism...or of laissez faire."

The *Lochner* era rolled on until 1937. The Supreme Court struck down laws outlawing contracts in which workers agreed not to join unions,[44] laws restricting courts' power to enjoin strikes,[45] laws mandating minimum wages[46] and maximum prices,[47] laws limiting competition,[48] and laws regulating the fees paid to employment agencies.[49]

As with the Supreme Court's use of the interstate commerce clause to curb federal regulatory laws, the *Lochner* era came to an abrupt end in 1937, in an opinion written by Chief Justice Charles Evans Hughes.

Charles Evans Hughes may have the most impressive resume in American history. In order he was a partner in a prominent New York law firm, the chairman of a commission that revolutionized the insurance industry, governor of New York, associate justice of the United States Supreme Court, Republican candidate for president in the 1916 election, secretary of state under Presidents Warren Harding and Calvin Coolidge, and Chief Justice of the United States. As Chief Justice, he looked the part. Handsome, white-maned, full-bearded, imposing, reserved, he looked like a latter-day Robert E. Lee. His performance was less impressive, marked by an inability to unify a fractious Court and a flexible approach to decision making that often looked like inconsistency. Still, he is considered one of the Court's great justices, and there was no equivocation in his opinion in *West Coast Hotel v. Parrish*, which rang down the curtain on the *Lochne*r era.[50]

In *Parrish*, the Court upheld a state's minimum wage law. It specifically overruled a number of earlier decisions, rejected freedom of contract as a liberty protected by the due process clause, and said that "regulation that is reasonable in relation to its subject and is adopted in the interests of the community is due process." Since 1937, the Supreme Court has never used substantive due process to strike down state economic legislation.

The *Lochner* era was down for the count. Substantive due process was not down for the count, but it was on the ropes. *Parrish* didn't directly address the use of substantive due process to protect personal liberties, but it was a mixed bag for liberals. On the one hand, it effectively stripped property and economic liberties of almost all constitutional protection, which they liked. On the other hand, it made it likely that the Court's friendly attitude toward economic legislation would carry over to state laws restricting personal liberties, for Hughes was clearly referring to regulation of all liberties, personal as well as economic, when he said that "regulation that is reasonable in relation to its subject is due process." Within a year, Justice Harlan Fiske Stone would guide the way out of this fix, giving liberals the best of both worlds. Before coming to Justice Stone and his famous footnote, however, we will pause to consider whether the Court was right in finding substantive protections in the due process clause.

It was clearly wrong.

Justice Bradley's *Slaughter-House* dissent and Chief Justice Morrison Waite's majority opinion in *Munn v. Illinois* both suggest that support for substantive due process can be found in ancient English laws, including the Magna Carta, that express broad concepts of liberty. The question, however, is not what "liberty" means in the due process clause, but what "due process" means, and these ancient laws do not address this question.

Substantive due process is at odds with the words and the obvious intent of the due process clause. In restricting the right of a state to deprive its citizens of life, liberty or property *without* due process of law, it acknowledges the power of the state to deprive them of life, liberty or property *with* due process of law. A state can deprive its citizens of all of the liberties to which the clause applies as long as it observes due process. In other words, the due process clause is not a limit on state power—it does not restrict what the states can do, but only how they do it. Substantive due process, on the other hand, restricts what the states can do. *Roe v. Wade*, for example, finds that the liberty protected by substantive due process includes the right to an abortion on demand for the first six months of the term, and holds that the state cannot deprive a woman of this right by any process—due, undue or in between. Substantive due process reflects a clear misreading of the due process clause.

In addition to this clear intent, there is contextual evidence in the Constitution that the due process clause is designed solely to assure procedural safeguards, not to confer substantive rights.

There is a due process clause in the Fifth Amendment, binding on the federal government. As Justice Felix Frankfurter said in his concurring opinion in *Adamson v. California*, the due process clause obviously means the same in the Fourteenth as in the Fifth Amendment.[51] In addition to the due process clause, the Fifth Amendment requires indictment by a grand jury, prohibits more than one prosecution for the same crime, confers a privilege against self-incrimination, and bans expropriation of property without compensation. Each of these rights is separated from its neighbors by semi-colons, with one exception. The exception is the self-incrimination privilege and the due process clause, linked in a passage stating that no person "shall be compelled in any criminal case to be a witness against himself, nor be deprived of life, liberty or property without due process of law." This use of a comma in a sea of semi-colons suggests that the self-incrimination privilege and the due process clause are kindred spirits, separated only by a friendly conjunction. Since the privilege against self-incrimination is procedural, limiting interrogation of witnesses in criminal proceedings, it is fair to assume that the due process clause is also procedural.

The background of the Fifth Amendment's due process clause also cuts against substantive due process. The Fifth Amendment was adopted immediately after the Constitution, and was proposed by the Founders. Substantive due process would limit to an unknown extent all of the powers conferred by the Constitution. It is *extremely* unlikely that the Founders contemplated this free-wheeling restriction on the powers they had so recently and carefully devised. It is also unlikely that they elected to give judges the sweeping authority needed to enforce a substantive due process restraint on federal legislative powers.

In 1938, the liberals' prospects for using substantive due process to advance their political and cultural agenda didn't look so good. Substantive due process was an indefensible doctrine, and the Supreme Court had just announced that it would almost never strike down state laws regulating the personal liberties that the liberals needed to advance their cause. And then along came Jones in the guise of Justice Harlan Fiske Stone, brandishing a footnote to save the damsel in distress.

Footnote Four—Revolution as Afterthought

Justice Harlan Fiske Stone was an unlikely revolutionary. Republican attorney general, Coolidge appointee to the Supreme Court, unprepossessing, jowly, portly, friendly and approachable—in his incognito travels, he often introduced himself simply as Harlan—he didn't seem the type. But in a footnote in the spiked milk case, he revolutionized the use of substantive due process.

In 1923, Congress passed a law excluding milk with certain additives from interstate commerce. Carolene Products Company challenged the law under both the interstate commerce clause and the Fifth Amendment's due process clause, and was shot down on both counts in Stone's 1938 opinion in *United States v. Carolene Products Co.*[52] In his due process discussion, Stone said that regulatory legislation would be presumed to be constitutional and would be upheld if it could show some rational basis for its existence. But then, to

73

protect liberties listed in the Bill of Rights from this standard of judicial review, Stone appends a footnote—the fourth footnote in his opinion—stating that "there may be narrower scope for this presumption of constitutionality" when the Court deals with state legislation restricting liberties protected by specific provisions of the Constitution, such as the Bill of Rights, even though, as discussed below, the Bill of Rights does not apply to the states.

The Bill of Rights is devoted almost exclusively to the protection of personal liberties. Stone's opinion thus adopts a preferred liberties approach to the due process clause, using it to protect the personal liberties covered by the Bill of Rights without placing significant limits on state control of economic activity or property rights.

In saying that there "may be" a reason to give Bill of Rights liberties a preferred status, Stone acknowledges that they had no such status at the time, and he was clearly right. Supreme Court decisions before 1937 did not favor Bill of Rights liberties over property rights. Quite the contrary. While the Court had occasionally used the due process clause to protect rights listed in the Bill of Rights, including freedom of speech, its property-protecting decisions came earlier, more frequently and with greater passion than its Bill of Rights cases. In 1922 the Court said that the due process clause did not protect freedom of speech.[53] Five years later, the Court changed its mind, but even then it gave the benefit of the doubt to state statutes impairing free speech, holding in *Whitney v. California* that laws restricting free speech would be upheld unless they are "arbitrary and unreasonable."[54]

Stone's preferred liberties approach finds no support in the words of the Fourteenth Amendment. That amendment commands simply that "no state may deprive any person of life, liberty or property without due process of law." These words subject liberty and property to the same due process restriction, and draw no distinction between economic and other liberties. Stone cites no background or history indicating that these words mean anything other than what they say.

Lacking support from both the Constitution and earlier cases, Stone simply conjures his preferred ordering of liberties out of thin air. Footnote 4 was judicial legislation, pure and simple. It has been very effective legislation, guiding the future development of the law. More importantly, it pulled substantive due process off the ropes, saving it to fight another day in the cause of the liberal version of truth, justice and the American way. And if revolution is defined as an abrupt, decisive change of direction, driven by emotion rather than reason, footnote 4 of *Carolene Products* is revolutionary. As a footnote, it is revolution as afterthought.

In constitutional law, footnote 4 has achieved rock star status. Its name has changed from footnote 4 to Footnote Four—the Fab Four?—and it commands a separate entry in *The Oxford Companion to the Supreme Court of the United States*.

But if Footnote Four is a rock star, it is only a warm-up act. It is somewhat tentative, stating that there "may be" a basis for preferring Bill of Rights liberties, and, as we have seen, it did not provide any justification of or constitutional foundation for the preferred liberties approach.

That fell to Justice Hugo LaFayette Black and his incorporation doctrine.

Incorporation Doctrine—The Leap of Illogic

You'd never know it from press accounts or recent Supreme Court decisions, but the Bill of Rights doesn't apply to the states. The First Amendment by its terms applies only to Congress, and John Marshall in *Barron v. Baltimore* held that the states were not bound by any of the other provisions of the Bill of Rights.[55]

Barron v. Baltimore was decided before adoption of the Fourteenth Amendment. Beginning with *Twining v. New Jersey* in 1908,[56] the Supreme Court often held that the liberties protected by the due process clause included many of those protected by the Bill of Rights. In *Gitlow v. New York*, the Supreme Court held that anarchist Benjamin Gitlow could be prosecuted for publishing tracts advocating the violent overthrow of the government, but it said that freedom of the press was a liberty protected by the Fourteenth Amendment.[57] (In one of history's many ironies, Gitlow ended up as a staunch, active conservative.) Other cases used the Fourteenth Amendment to protect freedoms of the press and religion. In *Powell v. Alabama*, the Court, responding to an Alabama justice system that had railroaded several young black men to a death sentence without benefit of counsel, held that the due process clause created a right of counsel in state capital cases, similar to the Sixth Amendment's right to counsel in federal criminal cases.[58]

Until the 1940s, the Supreme Court had used the Bill of Rights to identify liberties worthy of protection under the Fourteenth Amendment, but had not applied the Bill of Rights to the states. In *Twining*, the Court said that some Bill of Rights liberties applied under the due process clause, but added that they applied "not because they are enumerated in the [Bill of Rights], but because they are included in the conception of due process of law." In his dissent in *Gitlow*, Justice Holmes said that while "the general principle of free speech must be taken to be included in the Fourteenth Amendment," the states were probably not bound by the categorical "Congress shall pass no law" language in the First Amendment. And in his *Powell v. Alabama* opinion, Chief Justice Hughes relied primarily on ancient English law, not the Sixth Amendment.

There is a big difference between applying the Bill of Rights to the states and using the Bill of Rights to identify liberties protected by substantive due process, as we can see by using freedom of the press as an example. The First Amendment says that "Congress shall pass no law abridging the freedom of the press." If freedom of the press is a liberty protected by substantive due process, the due process clause in effect protects it by providing that "no state shall deprive any person of [freedom of the press] without due process of law." "Due process" is obviously a less demanding standard than "pass no law," giving the states much more leeway to restrict the press than Congress has under the First Amendment.

The distinction between using the Bill of Rights to identify liberties protected by substantive due process and applying the Bill of Rights to the states ended with Hugo Black.

Hugo Black was an Alabama senator and a strong supporter of the New Deal when Franklin Roosevelt tapped him for the Supreme Court in 1937. Following a slow start in which he was forced to explain his youthful membership in the Ku Klux Klan, Black settled into a 34 year career in which he became one of the most influential justices in the Court's history. Straddling the Roosevelt and Warren Courts, Black was the leader of and de facto spokesman for the liberal wings of both courts (at least until Chief Justice Earl Warren fully asserted himself). At his unwavering, oft-repeated urging, the Court adopted an expansive, almost absolutist reading of freedom of speech and press, construed the religious establishment clause in a way that now threatens to drive all vestiges of religion from the public square, outlawed prayers in public schools, mandated one-man, one-vote, and expanded the rights of the accused in criminal proceedings. As important as these things are in the development of constitutional law, Black's most important contribution to constitutional law is the incorporation doctrine.

It was Black's unique theory that the due process clause did not simply protect liberties identified in the Bill of Rights, but actually incorporated the Bill of Rights, making them applicable word for word to the states just as if the Bill of Rights applied directly to the states. The Supreme Court has never accepted Black's full incorporation theory, but it has incorporated most of the Bill of Rights, and it has generally done so in Black's word for word, apply the Bill of Rights directly to the states approach.[59] When the Supreme Court considers a state's alleged impairment of free speech, for example, it refers, not to the Fourteenth Amendment, but to the First Amendment.

The incorporation doctrine in an absurdity. As we have seen, there is a due process clause in the Bill of Rights, buried deep in the Fifth Amendment, and it means the same thing there as in the Fourteenth Amendment. The due process clause in the Bill of Rights obviously confers protections in addition to, and therefore different from, the other provisions of the Bill of Rights, so neither it nor the identical clause in the Fourteenth Amendment incorporates the other provisions of the Bill of Rights.

Freedom of speech is only one of the liberties protected by the due process clause. Let's assume that the Fourteenth Amendment said that "no state shall deprive any person of freedom of speech without due process of law." Nobody in his right mind would claim that this means the same as "Congress shall pass no law abridging the freedom of speech." So what the incorporation theorists are saying is that speech has greater protection as an unnamed liberty in the due process clause than it would have if it enjoyed specific constitutional protection! Conservatives need their own howling events to react to "reasoning" like this.

Beyond these analytical points lies the more obvious point that if Congress, in proposing the Fourteenth Amendment, had intended to apply the Bill of Rights to the states, it would have done so in plain English. It would not have relied on language so general and ambiguous that nobody claimed for 80 years after its adoption that it incorporated the Bill of Rights. It certainly would not have used a provision that was already a part, and a very small part, of the Bill of Rights. If a congressional staffer asked to draft a proposed constitutional amendment that applied the Bill of Rights to the states had responded with the due process clause, he would have been fired on the spot. If an 1880s law student had suggested in his final exam that the due process clause incorporated the Bill of Rights, he would have flunked the course.[60]

In his 1947 concurring opinion in *Adamson v. California*, Justice Felix Frankfurter, one of the Supreme Court's great justices, took the measure of the incorporation doctrine. In 70 years, he said, 43 judges, including the likes of Miller, Holmes, Louis Brandeis, Cardozo and Stone, had considered the scope of the Fourteenth Amendment. Many of these judges, he added, had been present at the creation of the Fourteenth Amendment. "Of all these judges," Frankfurter said, "only one, who may respectfully be called an eccentric exception, ever indicated a belief that the Fourteenth Amendment was a shorthand summary" of the Bill of Rights. Frankfurter summarily rejects both full incorporation and the partial incorporation that the Court has since adopted.[61]

The incorporation doctrine is a boon for liberals. Even more than Footnote Four, it confers preferred status on the specific personal liberties protected by the Bill of Rights while ignoring property rights. And by unconstitutionally subjecting the states to the exacting standards of the Bill of Rights, it allows liberals to use substantive due process to advance their political and cultural agenda free from interference from the states. Using the incorporated Bill of Rights, liberals have, among other things, struck down state attempts to restrict pornographic "literature," to protect their officials and public persons from libelous attacks, to prevent liberal domination and corruption of schools and colleges, and to promote religion and religious displays.

But Footnote Four and the incorporation doctrine didn't quite get the liberals all the way home. Neither Footnote Four nor the incorporation doctrine extends its sheltering arms to conduct, such as abortion, that doesn't fit into the categories of the Bill of Rights. Indeed, Footnote Four, which limits preferred status to liberties included in the Bill of Rights, raised a red flag. Enter, stage far left, Justice William O. Douglas and his right of privacy.

Right of Privacy—*Lochner* in Drag

William O. Douglas was a mean, miserable man, unloved by his ex-wives, his kids, his secretaries and law clerks, a host of estranged friends and many colleagues. Born in Minnesota, reared in Washington state, educated at Columbia Law School, he was a wunderkind—law school professor at 28, member of the Securities and Exchange Commission at 37, Supreme Court justice at 40. In a 36 year career on the Court, the longest in the Court's history, marred at the end by a refusal to retire despite repeated disabling strokes, he was a gadfly, feuding with fellow justices and often expounding extreme positions rejected by all the other justices. Generally paired with Black in the public mind, he lacked Black's humanity and sense of institutional restraint. A loner attracted to wilderness wanderings, he used his disdain for nuance and an elegant, pithy writing style to dash off his short opinions and head for the hills. When he was assigned *Griswold v. Connecticut*, the contraceptives case, his years in the wilderness became his day in the sun.

Douglas was determined to strike down Connecticut's ban on contraceptives, but as we saw in Chapter 1, the decision didn't come easy. The specific guarantees of the Bill of Rights weren't of much help, and it was in fact in this case that Justice Black cashed in his chips, arguing in a dissenting opinion that the due process clause did not protect a right of privacy.

Douglas was invited to return to the *Lochner* era, but he didn't want to take this tack for a number of reasons. *Lochner* was discredited, repeatedly rejected by the Supreme Court. A *Lochner* approach would invoke *Carolene Products*, with its presumption of constitutionality and its eagerness to uphold any statute that could show a "rational basis" for its existence, and Douglas did not want to set his lamb among those lions. Finally, an opinion based on *Lochner* would extend its protection to property and economic liberties, and Douglas was not a fan of property rights.

We have seen in Chapter 1 how Douglas solved his dilemma. Scouring the Bill of Rights, he found a right of privacy in its "penumbras, formed by emanations," and used these penumbras to smite the Connecticut statute.

Douglas' solution was brilliant. By giving his invention a name, and a fetching one at that—who could object to a right of privacy?—and lodging it in the Bill of Rights, he implicated both the incorporation doctrine and the concept of preferred liberties, without giving any support to property rights.

The Supreme Court has subsequently applied Douglas' right of privacy, most famously in *Roe v. Wade*, finding a constitutional right to abortion on demand for the first six months of pregnancy, but it has rejected his suggestion that the right of privacy could be shoe-horned into the Bill of Rights. Instead, it held in *Roe* that the right of privacy in general, and the right to an abortion in particular, were preferred "fundamental liberties" under substantive due process. Laws restricting these liberties, the Court said, did not enjoy a presumption of constitutionality, nor could they defend themselves by pointing to some rational basis for their existence. On the contrary, such laws would be struck down unless the states could show a "compelling state interest" for their existence.

Justice Harry Blackmun wrote the opinion in *Roe*. In an earlier life, Blackmun had been general counsel for the Mayo Clinic in Rochester, Minnesota. In the summer of 1972 he used Mayo's library to conduct research for his opinion. This background informed his opinion, but also probably colored his views.

Blackmun's opinion starts with the facts. England had criminalized abortion at all stages of pregnancy since 1803, although a 1967 act of Parliament allowed abortion to preserve the life or physical or mental health of the mother. In the United States, Connecticut criminalized abortion at all stages of the pregnancy in 1821, and New York followed suit in 1828. By 1840, eight states had similar laws. Between 1850 and 1900, most states criminalized abortion at all stages, and those laws remained on the books of most states when Roe was decided, although about one fourth of the states had recently enacted laws allowing abortion in certain circumstances. As recently as 1967, the American Medical Association had adopted a resolution endorsing the state laws, although it had modified its position in 1970. And while Blackmun neglects to mention it, the New York Legislature had passed a restrictive abortion law just months before the *Roe* decision, only to have it vetoed by Governor Nelson Rockefeller, whose family was a long-time supporter of Planned Parenthood.

To summarize: abortion had been illegal in England for 170 years, with some recent liberalization; it had been illegal in a couple of American states for 150 years, in many for 130 years, and in most for about 100 years, with these restrictions continuing even as Blackmun put pen to paper. The AMA had endorsed the states' position within the last five years. Just months before, the New York Legislature had passed a restrictive abortion law. Great evidence, Harry, for your position that there is a "fundamental right" to abortion on demand in American law!

But maybe the case will get better when you turn to the law, as you cite Supreme Court decisions strong enough to make a case for throwing out these long-standing, widely-accepted laws restricting conduct not protected by any specific constitutional provision.

Actually, when Blackmun turns to the law, the case gets even weaker. To support a constitutional right to abortion on demand, he cites cases involving freedom of speech, double jeopardy, restrictions on teaching in a foreign language, restrictions on religious schools, forced sterilization, school board elections, welfare residency requirements, work requirements for Seventh

Day Adventists on their Sabbath, illegal searches and seizures, and, of course, *Griswold's* penumbras and emanations. Not much that seems relevant to destruction of fetuses.

The whole concept of specially protected "fundamental liberties" not found in the Constitution was, when *Roe* was decided in 1973, still wet behind the ears, with scant support in earlier Supreme Court cases. Blackmun cites seven cases, including *Griswold*, to support this concept. None of the cases was decided before 1940, and only one before 1963. The 1940 case does not support the concept. It involves religious freedom, which is firmly embedded in the First Amendment. One of the remaining cases also involved religious freedom, and two are based on the equal protection clause, not the due process clause. That leaves only two cases besides *Griswold*, and one of these was decided just months before *Roe*. None of these cases has anything to do with abortion.

Harlan Fiske Stone would not buy *Roe's* concept of specially protected "fundamental liberties" not based on specific provisions in the Constitution. Footnote Four very specifically limits preferred status to liberties listed in the Constitution. Under *Carolene Products*, laws restricting abortion would be entitled to a presumption of constitutionality and the benefit of the rational basis analysis.

Stone is not the only big-time name from the Supreme Court's past who would have voted to uphold state abortion laws. We *know* that Black would have dissented from *Roe* as he did from *Griswold*, and Hughes' *Parrish* opinion puts him in the states' corner. With their respect for state power and sensitivity to the proper role of courts in a democratic society, it is highly likely that Frankfurter and Jackson and Cardozo and Holmes and Brandeis and Miller and all of the other giants of the Court would have rejected *Roe*. In fact, it is inconceivable that any Supreme Court before, say, 1960, would have voted to outlaw abortion restrictions.

Harry Blackmun is arrayed against these men of storied reputation and judicious mind. Blackmun is a hero to liberals, but he was so intellectually dishonest and bent on enacting his personal agenda that he was prepared to find capital punishment unconstitutional despite several provisions in the Constitution recognizing that both state and federal governments have the power to execute criminals.[62] (If Blackmun had had his way, he would be famous as the justice who held that the Constitution spared the life of the guilty and protected the destruction of the innocent.)

The decision in *Roe v. Wade* is rejected by the facts, lacks support in the law and spurns the wisdom of the elders. Other than that Mrs. Lincoln, how was the play?

To reach desired results, Douglas finagled and Blackmun ignored the facts and massaged the law. Their use of the right of privacy brings the Court back to *Lochner*, where fancy words and concepts—like "freedom of contract" and "right of privacy" and "fundamental liberties"—are used by the Court to implement its conception of policy in an area not addressed by the Constitution. It is instructive in this regard to compare the definition of liberty in the *Lochner* era with the definition of liberty in *Casey*, the case reaffirming *Roe*.

In his opinion in *Allgeyer v. Louisiana*, Justice Peckham, author of the *Lochner* opinion, says that the liberty referred to in the due process clause includes the right of a person "to be free in the enjoyment of all his faculties; to be free to use them in all lawful ways; to live and work where he will; to earn his livelihood in any lawful calling; to pursue any livelihood or avocation." In *Casey*, the Court says that "at the heart of liberty is the right to define one's own concept of existence, of

meaning of the universe and of the meaning of human life."
While these formulations differ in focus, they sound much the
same, neither is based on any specific provision in the
Constitution, and they are both mush, nothing more than cover
for the personal and policy preferences of at least five members
of the Supreme Court. The right of privacy is *Lochner* in drag.

With the right of privacy, liberals had run the constitutional
table. *Parrish* and *Carolene Products* destroyed all property
rights and economic liberties except for unpaid takings and
excessive punitive damages, and liberals could live with that as
long as they could define "taking" down to a nubbin, which
they have proceeded to do. Footnote Four and the incorporation
doctrine fastened the Bill of Rights on the states, assuring that
the states could do little to preserve cultural, moral or religious
values. The right of privacy strips states of their power to
restrict almost all private conduct, including abortion. The
liberals' entire social and cultural agenda has been enacted.
And best of all, it has been enacted by judicial legislators who
are unelected, not subject to recall, and institutionally reluctant
to change their minds.

Summary and Solutions

The Supreme Court's due process decisions reflect a
massive abuse of judicial power. First, to serve the dominant
economic forces of the day, the Court gives substantive content
to a clause designed only to assure procedural regularity and
safeguards. Then, at the dawn of the liberal era, the Court
weaves a preferred-liberties tapestry from whole cloth,
allowing it to protect personal liberties while keeping property
and economic liberties in their no-rightful place. Next, the
Court invents the cockamamie incorporation doctrine and uses

it to apply the Bill of Rights to the states, contrary to logic, history, clear language and its own prior decisions. Finally, to support those elements of the liberal social and cultural agenda that lie beyond the protective reach of Footnote Four and the incorporation doctrine, the Court revives the discredited *Lochner* approach, dusts it off, gussies it up, alters its appearance, changes its name to protect the guilty, and emerges with a so-called right of privacy whose best known offspring is an aborted fetus. And the conservatives have only themselves to blame, since they started it all with their invention of substantive due process. Stephen Field should be spinning in his grave.

What to do?

1. Scrap substantive due process? Deep-sixing substantive due process is maybe not so wild a dream. In the wake of *Parrish*, it was near death, saved only by Footnote Four, and it is now being used as irresponsibly as it was before 1937. It is thus only about 70 years old, and it should be in bad odor.

If the Supreme Court was unwilling to reject substantive due process in full, it could hold that there is no constitutional basis for substantive due process and reject the *Lochner*/right of privacy abuse of substantive due process. It could then go on to say that it would retain Footnote Four on the grounds that it was long-standing, that its foundation in specific provisions of the Constitution limited judicial discretion and abuse, and that both business and society had come to rely on it.

But this probably won't happen. The Supreme Court is probably unwilling to confront the liberal wailing and anguish that would greet even a partial rejection of substantive due process. We are likely stuck with substantive due process.

2. Revisit Roe v. Wade. With its present composition, the Supreme Court is unlikely to revisit *Roe v. Wade*, and would probably reaffirm it if it did—if Kennedy voted as he did in *Casey*, the vote would be 5-4 for no change even if Justices Roberts and Alito voted to overrule *Roe*. And it makes no sense to revisit *Roe* unless success is fairly certain, since if *Roe* is reaffirmed one more time, even the conservative justices might conclude that the issue is settled. On the other hand, if, as appears possible, President Bush is able to change the complexion of the Court, *Roe* should be ripe for another challenge.

In discussing the right of privacy I have explored *Roe's* disdain for the facts and creative use of the law, but a few more points are in order.

Since the right to privacy and *Roe v. Wade* are descendants of *Lochner*, lacking any specific support in the Constitution, a statute outlawing abortion should be entitled to *Carolene Products'* presumption of constitutionality and reasonable basis analysis. With the advance in scientific knowledge showing significant fetal development early in the term, coupled with the fact that a woman ordinarily doesn't know that she's pregnant until several weeks into the term, a state has a rational basis—protection of a developing, quickening fetus—to outlaw abortion.

A challenge to *Roe* would marshal the gathering evidence that a fetus suffers pain, and maybe even the horror of impending doom, during the abortion procedure. If a state can outlaw cruelty to animals, why not fetuses?

Roe emphasizes that abortion restrictions saddle women with unwanted children, but that ignores the humanity of the fetus and misstates the issue. The state does not allow a woman to kill or abandon her newborn if she decides on the delivery table that she does not want the child, and *Roe* itself allows abortion restrictions during the third trimester. The question is not whether the state can saddle a woman with an unwanted child, but when, and the Supreme Court has decided that it, rather than state legislatures, will make this policy decision.

And what about a woman's "control over her own body." *Roe* recognizes a woman's right to control her body, but then allows abortion restrictions during the third trimester, when the burdens of pregnancy are presumably the greatest and when the most painful point of child-bearing, delivery of the child, occurs. So here, as with the unwanted child position, there is no principle at work, but only a policy decision made by the court, determining the time at which a woman's control over her own body comes to an end.

The absurd claim that anti-abortion laws impose their moral values on others should be met head on. A fetus is undeniably life, whether or not philosophers can agree that it is a person, and the state regularly protects life far less substantial than a human fetus—like long-named flies and snail darters, for example. A developing fetus has a greater claim to humanity and to life itself than a fighting cock. Are we who are opposed to cock fighting and have made it illegal improperly imposing our values on those who would like to watch and bet on cock fights? In any event, the law regularly embodies morality— theft, murder and discrimination on the basis of race, ethnicity and sex are both illegal and immoral.

A challenge to *Roe* of course raises the question of whether there should be a more general challenge to the right of privacy. I think not, at least until a renewed challenge to *Roe* has been heard. In any event, I don't think that a blunderbuss attack on the right of privacy, as opposed to a case by case challenge to particular results, would be successful. If it keeps the concept of substantive due process, the Supreme Court is likely to reaffirm some of the decisions based on a right of privacy even if it abandons that right as a stated ground for decision, since under *Carolene Products* the issue in each case would be whether the challenged legislation can show some rational basis for its existence.

3. *Revive property rights.* In theory *Carolene Products* just gives states an edge in defending economic legislation, but in practice property and economic liberties are treated as second class citizens under the due process clause, and are denied all protection except for protection from unpaid taking, with "taking" very narrowly defined, and, within the last few years, protection from excessive punitive damage awards under the Eighth Amendment's ban on excessive fines.

There is no basis for limiting property rights to unpaid taking and excessive punitive damages. On the contrary, it is very clear that substantive due process protects property rights and economic liberties from state action beyond unpaid taking and excessive damages. The side-by-side positioning of the due process clause and the takings clause in the Fifth Amendment compels the conclusion that substantive due process protects property rights and economic liberties in addition to uncompensated expropriation and excessive damages. The *Casey* Court applied this reasoning—that substantive due process is meaningless if it is applied only to protect liberties already protected by other provisions in the Constitution—in asserting that the personal liberties protected by the due process clause are not limited to those specifically set forth in the Bill of Rights.

The words of the due process clause support revived protection for property and economic liberties. As we have seen, the due process clause is simply stated and easily understood, and it subjects property and liberty to the same due process standard and does not pick and choose among liberties. In fact, it doesn't apply to "liberties" at all. The root cause of all of the Court's misconstructions of the due process clause—the Footnote Four preference for Bill of Rights liberties, the incorporation doctrine, the "fundamental liberties" approach used to justify the right of privacy—is the Court's reading of the due process clause as though it protected "liberties," presumably discrete in number, sitting out there somewhere, waiting to be discovered, sorted, sifted and winnowed by the Supreme Court, with the Court to confer its protection on its self-chosen winners. But the due process clause does not protect "liberties"; it protects "liberty," a neutral concept embracing all human rights and activities, whether personal or economic, without giving preference to any of them.

This revived, properly understood property protection could be used to seek compensation for development rights and land value taken through regulatory expropriation. Under what's called the police power, a landowner can't claim compensation for value lost because use of his land is restricted by regulations, such as zoning ordinances, imposed to protect the value and use of neighboring property—if I build a steel plant in a residential neighborhood, my neighbors' land values and enjoyment of their properties will suffer. This regulation without compensation is legitimate. The same is not true of land use regulations such as restrictions on altering or demolishing historical structures or restrictions on developing endangered species habitat or wetlands, which are designed to serve the common good rather than to protect the neighborhood. If regulations imposed for the common good expropriate development rights and land values, why shouldn't the public pay for the taking, just as it does if it takes land for a public road? Applying the *Carolene Products* test, is there ever a "rational basis" for the state to take property without paying for it?

To focus this question in concrete terms, let's assume that the state decides to relocate a road to protect endangered species habitat, such as the hatching ground of the long-name fly. The state could not refuse to pay for the new road's right-of-way on the ground that it was needed to preserve the habitat, and yet it refuses to pay the owner whose development rights and property value are taken to preserve the habitat. Under a substantive due process that protects property rights beyond a right to payment for "taking" in a traditional sense, what "rational basis" is there to distinguish between the full expropriation for the road and the partial expropriation through land use restrictions?

4. *Challenge to the incorporation doctrine?* A reconstituted Supreme Court would almost certainly not scrap the preferred due process status of the liberties protected by the Bill of Rights, since that, like a rejection of substantive due process, would work a revolution in the law. Footnote Four is safe. The Court might, however, consider a challenge to the wacko incorporation doctrine, allowing the states some play in the joints as they cope with the Bill of Rights liberties, as Justice Holmes suggested in his *Gitlow* dissent.

There is one remaining issue under the due process clause—its use to impose the First Amendment's religious establishment clause on the states.

That issue deserves its own chapter.

CHAPTER 4

The Ungodly Abuse of the Establishment Clause

On June 27, 2005, we received law from on high, but it wasn't the Ten Commandments. And Lord knows it didn't come from Him.

The pronouncement came from the elevated bench of the United States Supreme Court, in an opinion in *McCreary County v. ACLU* written by Justice Souter on behalf of a 5-4 majority.[63] It booted the Ten Commandments from county courthouses, once again allowing a single judge to make law for a democratic nation of 300 million souls.

In *McCreary*, the county had adorned its courthouse walls with a "Foundation of American Law and Government Display" consisting of the Ten Commandments flanked by copies of the Magna Carta, Declaration of Independence, Bill of Rights, Star Spangled Banner, Mayflower Compact, National Motto (In God we Trust) and the Preamble of the Kentucky Constitution, and a picture of Lady Justice. Despite the Ten Commandments' secular companions, the Court upheld a lower court's order banning the Ten Commandments from the courthouse based upon a finding that the county's "manifest objective" was to promote religion. Under the religious establishment clause, the Court said, you cannot insist on being known by the company you keep.

But—and in establishment clause cases there is always a but, so conflicted are the majority justices—the Court, noting that a commandment-clutching Moses was among the lawgivers immortalized on the frieze in the Court's own courtroom, indicated that a religious display might pass muster if it was part of a secular cohort.

In another June 27 case, *Van Orden v Perry*, the Court found just such a cohort.[64] The 22 acre Texas capitol grounds hosts 17 monuments, including the Ten Commandments, and 21 historical markers. In this context, the four *McCreary* dissenters, joined by Justice Breyer from the *McCreary* majority, upheld the Ten Commandments monument on the basis that its religious nature was overshadowed by its historical significance in the midst of the other monuments and markers.

Justices Scalia and Thomas dissented in *McCreary* and concurred in *Van Orden*. Scalia said that the Court's establishment clause cases, including *McCreary* and *Van Orden*, do not involve an establishment of religion as that term was understood when the Bill of Rights was adopted. Thomas agreed, and then added that the establishment clause cannot be applied to the states even if it means what the Court says it means. Scalia was particularly caustic in his *McCreary* dissent, observing that "what distinguishes the rule of law from a dictatorship of a shifting Supreme Court majority is the absolutely indispensable requirement that judicial opinions be grounded in consistently applied principle." Both Scalia and Thomas are right, as we will see. First, though, we will place their opinions in judicial and historical context.

McCreary and *Van Orden* are only the latest in a long line of Supreme Court decisions responding to attacks on religious displays and endorsements. The Court's most recent prior establishment clause decision, *Zelman v. Simmons-Harris*, delivered on the last day of the Court's 2001-2002 term, involved state aid to religious schools, the other bountiful source of establishment clause litigation.[65]

The Cleveland public schools were a dysfunctional basket case. For a generation and more, they had been among the worst schools in the country. They failed to meet all statewide performance standards. Over two thirds of their students dropped or flunked out, and only 10 percent of their ninth graders could pass basic proficiency exams. In a sure sign that students were just shuffled along, 25 percent of their high school seniors failed to graduate.

In 1995, the courts stepped in, placing the Cleveland school district under state control. Ohio responded with an array of assistance to Cleveland students, including public community and magnet schools and a voucher program for students who chose to attend religious or non-religious private schools.

The voucher program was challenged under the First Amendment ban on laws "respecting an establishment of religion," generally known as the establishment clause. The challenge was upheld by the federal district court and the federal court of appeals, but was rejected by the Supreme Court in *Zelmam*.

Citing a long line of cases, the majority upheld the voucher program because the aid was given to students who were free to use it at either religious or non-religious schools, rather than directly to the religious schools. The vouchers were a tool to provide education to students in a failed system, a legitimate secular purpose, and were not an aid to religion. The fact that 96 percent of the voucher students chose parochial schools, cited by the dissenters as evidence of state aid to religion, was dismissed by the majority on the grounds that multiple private choices don't add up to state action and that the ratio of religious to non-religious aid drops sharply when the voucher program is thrown in with the other programs, including community and magnet schools, that Ohio adopted in response to the Cleveland crisis.

Zelman breathes life into the voucher movement, allowing its supporters to go to the states freed from the threat of and resort to federal judicial power that have been used by voucher opponents to discourage adoption of voucher programs and to attack those that have been adopted. The federal courts no longer pose a threat to state and federal use of vouchers to rescue students in failing schools and to generate a healthy competition with public schools.

Useful as vouchers are, however, there are limits to the benefits they can deliver. Individually directed aid generally provides no capital funds to the recipient schools, and it provides an unpredictable source of operating funds that is subject to change from semester to semester, making it difficult if not impossible for the recipient schools to base enrollment, staffing, capital funding and other decisions on the public aid. A voucher program would be more effective if it could be coupled with direct public aid to religious schools, providing them with a relatively secure and predictable source of operating and capital funds that would enhance their ability to compete with the public schools for voucher and non-voucher students.

Under *Zelman* and other establishment clause cases, direct public aid to parochial schools is not an available option. Aid funneled through students or parents is acceptable, but direct aid is not. The federal courts have thus erected an impassable roadblock to the use of direct aid as a supplement to vouchers.

There is nothing in the establishment clause or the due process clause that bans either direct state aid to parochial schools or courthouse postings of the Ten Commandments. The courts are wrong on the law, basing their position on a misreading of the establishment clause and its applications to the states.

Wall of Separation–The Law of the Letter

The first case to apply the establishment clause to the states was *Everson v Board of Education*, decided in 1947. In that case, Justice Hugo Black, quoting an 1802 letter in which Thomas Jefferson said that the establishment clause imposed a "wall of separation" between church and state, said that a state could not pass any laws that aid religion. Based upon *Everson*, the courts have consistently struck down laws that aid or endorse religion or religious expression.

Basing constitutional law on the offhand comments of famous people is dangerous, and this is particularly true of Jefferson. Jefferson was a great and generally a wise man, but in his private actions he was often outrageous and irresponsible. Advocating violent revolution each generation, he said that "the tree of liberty must be refreshed from time to time with the blood of patriots and tyrants." Emotionally and politically wedded to the French Revolution, in a letter written when he was the United States Secretary of State he justified the Jacobin bloodbath with the observation that "I would [see] half the earth desolated. Were there but an Adam and an Eve left in every continent, and left free, it would be better than it is now." While Vice President of the United States, bound by a solemn oath to the Constitution, he secretly authored a resolution enacted by the Kentucky legislature that asserted that states had a "natural right" to nullify federal laws. And he was a zealot on the separation of church and state. The inscription on his tomb, which he wrote, announces that he authored the Virginia Statute for Religious Freedom, but fails to note that he was President of the United States.

The "wall of separation" was thus constructed by a suspect builder, but that is just the beginning of its problems. The establishment clause cases built upon the wall of separation provide exquisite proof of Justice Holmes' theorem that "general propositions do not decide concrete cases." In *Everson* itself, the Court, with Black writing for the majority, split 5-4 in upholding a New Jersey statute providing transportation reimbursement to parochial school students, showing that the nine judges agreed that there was a wall, but didn't know where it was. The post-*Everson* cases could not have been predicted by and cannot be explained or reconciled by the wall of separation metaphor or any other governing principle. Among other things, the courts have held that it is acceptable to bus parochial school students to class, but not on field trips; that the states may pay for diagnostic services in religious schools, but not therapeutic services; that the states can give parochial schools books that contain maps, but not the maps themselves; that a creche is okay if it is part of a Christmas exhibit, but not if it stands alone; that a menorah is okay, but a creche is not; that a state may provide speech and hearing tests in religious schools, but not speech and hearing services; that the states can lend textbooks to a parochial school, but not a film or film projector; that textbooks can be lent to parochial schools if they are returned unaltered, but not if students have written in them; that the state can pay parochial schools for state written tests, but not for teacher-prepared tests on non-religious topics;[66] and that, as we have seen, the Ten Commandments are okay if they are lost in a secular crowd assembled with a good intent, but not if they are lost in a secular crowd assembled with a bad intent. (The opinions in these cases tend to be interminable, proving that the strength of an argument is adversely proportional to the number of words used to advance and support it.)

Even when the Supreme Court agrees that there has been a violation of the establishment clause, its majority members often do not agree why they agree. In Chapter 1, I quoted the Supreme Court's syllabus in *County of Allegheny v. ACLU*, introducing the welter of opinions in the 5-4, Solomonic decision that split the baby to allow a menorah but not a creche. The opinions in that case spotlight five fog-bound, policy-oriented judges vainly and separately searching for a wall of separation in a landscape teeming with secondary sources and prior opinions but no Constitution.

In an apparent attempt to dig itself out of this hole, the Supreme Court attempted in the aptly-named *Lemon* decision to provide a three-pronged analytical framework for its establishment clause decisions.[67] In *Lemon*, the Court struck down Pennsylvania and Rhode Island laws providing aid for secular courses taught at parochial schools. Attempting to harmonize and synthesize its prior holdings, the Court said that religious-based state assistance will be upheld only if it is secular in intent, secular in effect, and does not entangle the state with religion. The challenged laws, it held, violated the third prong of the three part test because the states had to get involved with the parochial school classes in order to assure that the aid was not used for religious purposes.

The Court should have heeded the adage that, if you're in a hole, stop digging. *Lemon* takes *Everson* and makes it even worse.

The middle of the three tines in the *Lemon* pitchfork—the requirement of secular effect—is just another way of embracing the wall of separation, for it spears any and all state action that aids or endorses religion. The other two tines—a secular motive, whether or not the effect is secular, and a lack of entanglement—build the wall even higher.

The pure motive requirement departs from the Supreme Court's general insistence that it will ignore legislative motive. In the *Heart of Atlanta* decision, for example, the Court upheld the Civil Rights Act of 1964 under the interstate commerce clause even though it acknowledged that the act may have been prompted by an urge for social justice.[68] Apparently motive is irrelevant when the Supreme Court considers liberal legislation, but not when it considers conservative legislation.

The difference between *Heart of Atlanta* and the establishment clause cases is highlighted by McCreary. In *McCreary*, the Ten Commandments were surrounded by a host of secular documents. Five of the commandments condemn conduct that is criminalized under the law of most states, while two—the injunctions to love thy father and mother and not to covet—express widely accepted, non-religious ethical precepts. Beyond that, as the majority in *Van Orden* recognizes, the Ten Commandments have undeniable historical significance. All in all, a strong case could be made that the county in good faith placed the commandments in a secular and historical context. But a majority of the Court, weighing evidence as though it were a court of common pleas, found a religious motive, and used that motive to banish the commandments. In *Heart of Atlanta,* the Court says it's okay for social justice to masquerade as commercial regulation. *In McCreary*, it holds that a suspect motive trumps a secular effect.

The "no entanglement" tine of the pitchfork is laughable in view of the law summarized above. Of the three bodies of government—legislative, executive and judicial—only one branch has "entangled" itself in religion, and it is not the legislative or executive branch.

As a guide for decision, the wall of separation metaphor, with or without the *Lemon* additions, has been a disaster. It is not grounded in the language or history of the establishment clause, and it is impossible to apply. In practice, it is simply a fount of judicial policy preferences and power. And as the Ninth Circuit's rejection of "under God" in the Pledge of Allegiance demonstrates, it is a corrupting power, unfettered by historical perspective, sense of proportion, reason, wisdom, judgment or common sense.

It was of course a mistake from the start to use the metaphor as the basis for applying the establishment clause. No responsible historian would use a casual, after-the-fact comment from a known partisan to divine the meaning of a constitutional provision. To determine what the establishment clause ban on establishment of religion is, we need to determine what an "establishment of religion" was when the clause was ratified as part of the Bill of Rights in 1791.

Establishment of Religion—Finding the Founders

In 1791, a few of the states imposed taxes for the support of churches. Some supported a single preferred church, while others made the support available to all churches, or to all Protestant churches. Most provided non-preferential support.[69]

Even as the establishments persisted, however, their days were numbered. One by one they fell to the liberalizing impulses born of the American Revolution, continuing a movement that began during the Revolution. In 1776, New Jersey had adopted a constitution providing that "no person shall be obliged to pay tithes, taxes or other rates, for the purpose of building or repairing any…church or churches, place or places of worship, or for the maintenance of any minister or ministry." In that same year, North Carolina's constitution provided that no person shall be compelled to "pay for the purchase of any glebe, or the building of any house of worship, or for the maintaining of any minister or ministry," and Pennsylvania's constitution stated that "no man ought to be compelled to…erect or support any place of worship or maintain any ministry." Vermont's 1777 constitution prohibited support of "any place of worship or ministry." The Virginia Statute for Religious Freedom, adopted in 1786, stated that "no man shall be compelled to support any religious worship, place or ministry." Delaware adopted Pennsylvania's disestablishment provision in 1792, and in 1798 Georgia adopted the New Jersey formulation. In 1810 Maryland prohibited taxes for the support of any religions, and Connecticut in 1818 decreed that "no one shall be compelled to support any religious society."[70]

The establishments and disestablishments of religion immediately preceding and following adoption of the establishment clause disclose that, whether defined by friend or foe, an "establishment of religion" in 1791 was the targeted use of tax dollars to provide structural and operational support to organized religious groups in pursuit of their core missions of ministering to the faithful and reaching out to the heathens, with no secular purpose being served. This is the meaning recognized even by Jefferson's Statute for Religious Freedom, which, far from erecting a wall against all aid to or endorsement of religion, outlawed only support for "religious worship, place or ministry." It is a meaning that Jefferson acknowledged in action if not in words, for he advocated use of public funds for a school of theology, suggested that a room at the University of Virginia be set aside for religious services, and allowed the establishment of independent religious schools within the University of Virginia campus.[71] It is a meaning, moreover, that survived long after the establishment clause was adopted. Wisconsin's 1848 constitution states that no man "shall be compelled to...support any place of worship, or to maintain any ministry," and Minnesota's 1857 constitution contains a virtually identical provision.

None of the laws or actions struck down by the courts fit within this definition. Religious schools provide a primarily secular education recognized by states, colleges and employers. They provide the same secular education as public schools, and often do it better. Direct state aid to parochial schools thus serves a secular purpose. It provides no structural support to churches or ministries, and any operational support to religion is limited and incidental and directed more to religious education than to ministry.

Other things struck down by the courts fall even farther from the establishment tree. Manger scene exhibits, Ten Commandments displays and voluntary recitals of the Pledge of Allegiance are largely ceremonial and are at worst general endorsements or expression of religious belief that require virtually no tax dollars and provide no support of any kind to any organized religious group.

Apologists for the establishment clause decisions point out that the clause bans all laws "respecting" an establishment of religion and argue that "respecting " reaches everything that could aid or endorse religion. This is an absurd argument.

The dictionary defines "respecting" as "concerning" or "relating to." The establishment clause thus bans Congress from passing laws that relate to an establishment of religion. This can mean one of two things. It could mean that Congress can pass no law tinkering or interfering with state establishments of religion, many of which remained when the establishment clause was proposed in 1789, and there are those who argue that it was designed to do just that. Alternatively, it could mean that Congress can pass no law which tends toward the creation of an establishment of religion, or provides a component of an establishment of religion.

What is clearly not permitted by this language is a reading that writes "establishment" out of the establishment clause. Establishment was, in 1789, a term of art, with a well-recognized meaning, and no responsible reading of the establishment clause can ignore its presence. Yet that is exactly what the Supreme Court's decisions and their apologists do. They construe and apply the establishment clause as though it prohibited Congress from passing "any law respecting religion."

The laws, displays and actions impaled in the name of the establishment clause do not tend toward the creation of, and are not constituent parts of, an establishment of religion. We don't need wise men to lead us to the conclusion that 1,000 (or 10,000) manger scenes or Ten Commandments postings do not establish a church, and state aid to parochial schools retains its secular character, purpose and effect whether it is provided by one state or fifty (or by the federal government.).

Nativity scenes, publicly displayed Ten Commandments, "under God" in the Pledge of Allegiance, opening prayers in

Congress and the like undoubtedly convey an endorsement of or support for religion that offends some people (mainly People for the American Way). These religious endorsements are not coercive, however. Unlike required school prayers or restrictions on religious practice, for example, they do not require anyone to do or to refrain from doing anything. Some people just don't like them. One has no constitutional right to be free from state conduct that he finds offensive but does not otherwise affect him. Some people object to use of their tax dollars to wage war or perform abortions. Most conservatives are offended by, among other things, officially-sanctioned racial and ethnic preferences, liberal bias in the public schools, the repressive, politically-correct conformity that many public universities impose upon their students in the name of diversity, and the imposition of this conformity by political faculties so politically and culturally non-diverse that less than five percent of their faculties are conservative.[72] ACLU members have no more right to be shielded from offensive government action than, say, members of the Christian Majority.

We can see the true offense-avoiding function of the establishment clause cases if we look at a couple of examples from Richmond, Virginia. The City of Richmond has erected a statue of Lincoln just outside the Tredegar Iron Works, the Confederacy's main arsenal, and a statue of Arthur Ashe, the black tennis player, just beyond the statues of the confederate heroes on Monument Row. These statues were, to put it mildly, controversial, seemingly a fewer-than-full-fingered salute to the Lost Cause. Let's assume that Richmond puts a manger scene on one side of Lincoln and Ashe and a Ten Commandments tablet on the other. The Daughters of the Confederacy object to Lincoln and Ashe, while the ACLU wants to get rid of the creche and the Ten Commandments.

Why on earth should the ACLU gets its way with the Supreme Court while the Daughters are told to take a hike?

The ACLU would no doubt respond that religion differs from other beliefs because of its power to intimidate non-believers and excluded groups. If this was ever true, it is not true now. Today, the demands of political correctness and group sensitivity are far more intimidating than the beleaguered and furiously-assaulted efforts of those who look to religion to inform political decisions and mold cultural values. In this age of political correctness, those who put Ashe and Lincoln on their pedestals are far more powerful than those who might seek to flank them with religious displays.

The Supreme Court's error in determining the scope of the establishment clause is compounded by a further error. Almost all cases that have arisen under the establishment clause, including the Pledge of Allegiance case, involve state, as opposed to federal, action. Even if the establishment clause prohibited all government aid to or endorsement of religion, as the Supreme Court claims, there is no basis to impose that prohibition on the states.

Incorporating the Establishment Clause— The Worst of a Bad Deal

In *Everson*, Justice Black used the incorporation doctrine to apply the establishment clause to the states. In Chapter 3, we have seen how ridiculous the incorporation doctrine is. But even if the due process clause did incorporate and apply to the states those provisions of the Bill of Rights that protect individual liberties, the incorporation would not include the establishment clause.

The due process clause states that no state may "deprive any person of liberty without due process of law." The clause applies only if a *person* is *deprived* of *liberty*.

Voltaire observed that the Holy Roman Empire was neither holy nor Roman nor an empire. The things struck down by the courts under the establishment clause involve neither a person nor a deprivation nor a liberty.

A manger scene or a Ten Commandments tablet just sit there. No " person" is speaking, or being spoken to, or otherwise affected. So, too, with aid to religious schools. A state sends money to the religious schools, which mingle those funds with their other funds and use them for educational purposes. No non-official "person" is involved. Public support for or endorsement of religion, with no coercive element, does not affect any individual "person."

There is no deprivation because nobody is forced to do or not to do anything, other than to see a little of his tax dollars spent on something to which he may object, and as we have seen, an objectionable expenditure of public funds does not amount to a constitutional injury.

The lack of deprivation is apparent from the wording of the First Amendment. That amendment says that Congress shall make no laws "prohibiting" the free exercise of religion, "abridging" freedom of speech, or "respecting" an establishment of religion. "Prohibiting" bespeaks deprivation. So does "abridging." "Respecting" does not.

No "liberty" is affected by the things that the courts have struck down or prohibited in the name of the establishment clause. "Liberty" is defined as being "free from restriction or control." Aid to religious schools and religious displays and endorsements impose no restrictions or control of any kind.

During one of his classes, I discussed this matter with Professor Laurence Tribe of Harvard Law School, an extremely liberal constitutional law professor and scholar. He agreed, based on the analysis made here, that there is no justification for using the incorporation doctrine to apply the establishment clause to the states through the due process clause.

James G. Blaine, one of the sponsors of the due process clause, plus lots of others who voted to propose or ratify the clause, concur.

Blaine was a Maine congressman and senator, speaker of the House of Representatives, secretary of state under three presidents, and 1884 Republican candidate for president in one of the Nation's first mud-slinging campaigns. Accused of shading the truth, Blaine was tagged by Democrats as "Blaine, Blaine, James G. Blaine. The continental liar from the state of Maine." Responding in kind against Democrat candidate Grover Cleveland, who had sired an out-of-wedlock child, Republicans asked "Ma, Ma, where's Pa? Gone to the White House. Ha! Ha! Ha!" Pa won, married in the White House, and fathered a baby Ruth who may or may not have inspired a candy bar.

In Congress, Blaine pushed for adoption of the Fourteenth Amendment, including the due process clause. Congress approved the amendment in 1866, and the states ratified it in 1868. Seven years later, Blaine proposed a constitutional amendment stating, among other things, that "no state shall make any law respecting an establishment of religion." Congress rejected the proposed amendment. Like Blaine, many of the other congressmen who voted on the Blaine amendment were in Congress when the due process clause was approved. Even those new to Congress in 1875 were presumably politically active adults in 1866. Thus the congressmen voting in 1875 were aware of the background of the due process clause and the tenor of the debates that attended its adoption by Congress and ratification by the states. Leonard Levy, who studied the debates on the Blaine amendment and who generally supports the Supreme Court's incorporation of the establishment clause, says that "the [proposed Blaine amendment] itself as well as comments made during the debates [on the amendment] demonstrated without doubt that the framers of the Fourteenth [Amendment] had not meant to apply the establishment clause to the states."[73]

Under the Constitution, a constitutional amendment proposed by Congress requires ratification by three fourths of the states. Following defeat of the Blaine amendment a number of states, including most of the states that had ratified the due process clause, amended their constitutions to specifically prohibit aid to religious organizations and institutions. These amendments were of course unnecessary if, as the Supreme Court held in 1947, the due process clause from its ratification in 1868 prevented the states from giving aid and comfort to religion. The legislators adopting these state law amendments were in 1868 either members of the ratifying legislatures or adults who were well aware of the background and debates on the due process clause. In adopting the Blaine-type restrictions, these legislators were therefore providing informed testimony that the due process clause did not in fact impose restrictions on religion.

A fair summary of this historical background is as follows. Both Congress and the ratifying states, informed by personal knowledge and experience, offer contemporaneous testimony that the establishment clause does not apply to the states through the due process clause. This testimony rings true, for the due process clause was presumably adopted to protect the recently-freed slaves, not to keep manger scenes and the Ten Commandments out of public places or to charge the Supreme Court with the high mission of finding the constitutionally significant differences between textbooks and maps, busing to classes and busing on field trips, and diagnostic and therapeutic services. The 1947 Supreme Court, composed of members the oldest of whom (Felix Frankfurter) was born in Europe 14 years after the due process clause was ratified, ignores this testimony and decides, without examining the history of the due process clause or the intention of those who proposed and ratified it, that the due process clause incorporates the establishment clause. Whatever one's view of elected officials may be, it is easy to give the palm to the legislators in this face off between the legislative and judicial branches.

As stated in Chapter 3, the Supreme Court has incorporated most but not all of the Bill of Rights into the due process clause. It has not incorporated the Second Amendment right to bear arms—not surprisingly, since this amendment is not favored by the ACLU—, the Fifth Amendment right to indictment by a grand jury, or any of the provisions of the Seventh Amendment, which requires certain procedures for non-criminal trials.[74] The Supreme Court should scrap the entire incorporation doctrine, but even if it does not do so, it could readily disincorporate the establishment clause consistent with its decision to incorporate only some of the provisions of the Bill of Rights.

Everson and its descendants are based upon bad law and worse history. They reflect an abuse of federal judicial power even more far-ranging than the abuses described in Chapter 3. The abuses chronicled in Chapter 3, outrageous as they are, involve only misconstructions of the due process clause. *Everson* and its followers misconstrue both the due process clause and the establishment clause, and to top it off, they misuse a misuser, applying the cockamamie incorporation doctrine in circumstances in which it doesn't apply even if you buy the doctrine in the first place. The real world consequences of all this is that in 1989, in *County of Allegheny v. ACLU*, we have nine grown men and women, the highest judicial officers in the land, using 107 pages in the United States Reports to decide whether the language that "no state shall deprive any person of liberty without due process of law" permits a menorah but not a creche, or a creche but not a menorah, or both, or neither, or whatever. This is worse than absurd. It is worse than ridiculous. It is just plain crazy!

The Supreme Court should overrule *Everson* and its befuddled followers. They have much less going for them than many of the cases the Supreme Court has in the past dumped in history's dustbin. The question is whether five justices could be persuaded now or in the near future to haul the Court's establishment clause cases to the dustbin.

There is reason for hope. In the other areas we have discussed, the justices will have to reorient their thinking—"disenthrall themselves," in Lincoln's words—in order to return to the Constitution. Here, on the contrary, the majority needed to inter the establishment cases may be within reach without drastic change in the law as expressed by a near-majority of justices. The late Chief Justice Rehnquist and three of the current justices on the Court have expressed a decided hostility to the establishment clause cases. In his dissent in *Wallace v Jaffree*, which banned a voluntary moment of silence in public schools, Rehnquist stated that the purpose of the establishment clause was to prevent establishment of a single preferred church. While technically wrong on his history—it appears that the establishment clause was designed to prevent establishment of multiple churches as well as a preferred church—Rehnquist's opinion shows that he recognizes the limited scope of the establishment clause. In a 1990 concurring opinion (*Westridge Community Board of Education v. Mergens*), Justice Anthony Kennedy, joined by Justice Antonin Scalia, said that there is no establishment of religion unless (i) government "gives direct benefit to religion in such a degree that it in fact establishes a state religion or religious faith, or tends to do so," and (ii) there is coercion of individuals.[75] As we have seen, in *McCreary* and *Van Orden* Scalia, joined by Kennedy and Thomas, said that the Supreme Court had misapplied the establishment clause, while Thomas said that, whatever the clause means, it doesn't apply to the states. Justice White dissented in *Jaffree*, stating that he "would support a basic reconsideration" of the establishment clause cases, and while White is no longer on the Court—he retired in 1993 and died in 2002—his dissent confirms that the Rehnquist-Kennedy-Scalia-Thomas views have mainstream support.[76] If Justices Roberts and Alito join the Rehnquist-Kennedy-Scalia-Thomas-White camp, the federal courts will be relieved of their religion police duties.[77]

CHAPTER 5

Bush and Gore in Florida —
The Wait of the World

At daybreak on November 8, 2000, George W. Bush led Al
Gore in Florida by 1784 votes out of nearly six million cast,
with all but the overseas ballots counted. Each candidate
needed Florida's 25 electoral votes to become president. With
the presidency in the balance, the Florida margin precipitated
36 days of contest, contention and indecision that consumed
the media, roiled the public, roused the passions and the fury of
the partisans, and bore the wait of the world. It is a story that has
been and will continue to be told and retold, vying for historical
place with the contested elections of 1800, 1824 and 1876. As
in the earlier chapters, a court is the villain of the piece, but in
this case it is the Supreme Court of Florida (Scofla), not the
Supreme Court of the United States (Scotus).

Background: Counters and Courts

Florida law requires a machine recount if the winning
margin is less than one-half of one percent. The statewide,
county-by-county recount began on November 8 and

proceeded slowly, with the news media snaring viewers and creating suspense by reporting dribbled-in results that showed Gore gaining on Bush. At the end of the recounts on November 10, the Bush lead had dwindled to a little more than 300 votes. Gore asked for a manual recount in Volusia, Palm Beach, Broward and Miami-Dade counties, each of which had gone heavily for Gore on Election Day.

Following a partial recount mandated by statute, the Palm Beach County canvassing board asked Katherine Harris, the Republican secretary of state who had been active in the Bush campaign, whether it could conduct a manual recount of all votes. She said no. The Democrat attorney general, who chaired Gore's Florida campaign, said it could conduct a manual recount. The canvassing boards in the four counties, all controlled by Democrats, elected to proceed with the manual recounts.

The recounted ballots included so-called "undervotes." Three of the counties employed punch card ballots in which the voter uses a stylus to detach a perforated "chad" opposite a candidate's name. Machines tabulate the votes by detecting light passing through the hole created by the stylus. If a ballot registers no vote for an office, it is an undervote for that office. The majority of the undervotes are on ballots on which there is no detachment of or indentation on the chad for the office. Some of the non-counted ballots, however, contain partiallly detached, or "hanging," chads, and some contain wholly attached "dimpled" chads that are indented in some manner. The canvassing boards examined hanging and dimpled chads to determine whether they should be counted as votes.

The Florida statutes state that the county canvassing boards "must" certify their returns to the secretary of state by no later than November 14 (seven days after the election), but then provide that the secretary "may" ignore late filed returns. It takes time to count dimpled chads, and the seven-day deadline loomed with the recounts far from complete. Harris said she would not accept late-filed returns. Gore applied to Judge Terry Lewis in Leon County for an order compelling Harris to accept late returns. Lewis held that Florida law required the returns to be filed by November 14, but that Harris had to justify any refusal to accept amended returns filed after November 14.

Harris ordered the canvassing boards to explain why they needed more time. After receiving their explanations, she again refused to accept returns filed after November 14, and Judge Lewis upheld her decision. Volusia County completed its recount by November 14. The other three counties did not. They submitted returns on November 14 based upon the machine recount, and then continued their manual recounts.

Gore appealed Lewis' decision to Scofla. In an opinion delivered November 21 (Scofla I), Scofla reversed Lewis and ordered Harris to accept recount returns filed by 5 p.m. Sunday, November 26, with the recounts continuing in the meantime.[78] Despite the discretion seemingly conferred on Harris by the provision that she "may" accept late-filed returns, Scofla held that she was required by law to accept late-filed returns. Bush asked Scotus to review Scofla I. On November 24, Scotus agreed to hear the appeal.

In the meantime, the recounts continued, kind of. Broward County completed its recount before November 26. Palm Beach County completed its recount, but missed the Scofla deadline by several hours. Miami-Dade counted most of the day on November 22, but then stopped counting, saying that it could not complete the count by the Scofla deadline.

In the late evening of November 26, the Florida Canvassing Commission certified Bush the winner by 537 votes, which included the overseas ballots. The commission accepted the Broward recount but rejected the Palm Beach recount and refused to include the votes counted in Miami-Dade's partial recount.

On November 27, Gore brought a "contest" action in the Leon County trial court challenging the certification on the grounds, among others, that the certified vote count did not include the results of the full Palm Beach or partial Miami-Dade recounts or a review of the undervotes in Miami-Dade County that had not been counted manually. The case was assigned to Judge N. Sanders Sauls, who took testimony on December 2 and 3 and ruled from the bench on December 4, denying all relief requested by Gore. Gore appealed to Scofla.

On the same day that Judge Sauls rendered his decision, Scotus delivered its opinion (Scotus I) in the appeal from Scofla I.[79] In a brief, unanimous opinion, the Court said that it could not tell from Scofla I whether Scofla had considered the effect of Article II, Section 1 of the United States Constitution, which provides that presidential electors shall be appointed in such manner as the state legislatures may direct, and 3 United States Code Section 5, which deprives presidential electors of "safe harbor" protection from congressional challenge unless the electors are appointed in accordance with laws enacted before the election. It seemed possible, the Court suggested, that Scofla had not followed statutory law in effect on Election Day, thereby violating the federal constitution and jeopardizing the Florida electors' safe harbor status. The Court vacated Scofla I and sent the case back to Scofla.

On December 7, Scofla heard the appeal from Judge Sauls' decision, and on December 8 it delivered a 4-3 opinion (Scofla II) that largely reversed Sauls.[80] It held that the Gore vote totals in the Palm Beach recount and Miami-Dade partial recount had to be included in Gore's column, and it ordered an immediate manual recount of all undervotes in the state that had not been manually counted, with the count to be conducted by unnamed public officials. It did not set any standards by which the dimpled chads were to be counted. Bush immediately asked Scotus to review Scofla II and to stay any further counting until Scotus had heard and decided the case.

Upon receipt of Scofla II, Judge Sauls removed himself and was immediately replaced by Judge Lewis, who ordered a statewide recount of undervotes to begin immediately and to be completed by the late afternoon of December 10. The recount began the morning of December 9. That afternoon Scotus stayed all further counting, agreed to review Scofla II, and set a hearing for December 11.

Scotus heard the case on December 11 and delivered its decision (Scotus II) late in the evening of December 12.[81] There were six opinions. A majority of the Court (Rehnquist, O'Connor, Scalia, Kennedy and Thomas) held that Scofla's standardless recount violated the Fourteenth Amendment's equal protection clause because voters in different counties would be subject to different standards, and it concluded that there was no time for further counting because the December 12 deadline for resolving disputes under the safe harbor statute was "upon us." Three justices (Rehnquist, Scalia and Thomas) joined the majority opinion and delivered a concurring opinion in which they said they would have reversed Scofla II on a number of other grounds. Souter and Breyer agreed that a standardless recount would violate the equal protection clause, but they said that the real deadline was December 18, when the electors were scheduled to vote, rather than December 12, and suggested that there was enough time before December 18 to develop a standard and recount the votes. Justices Stevens and Ginsburg would have affirmed Scofla II.

Scotus II ended the election contest. After sleeping on the decision, Gore conceded at 8 p.m. on December 13, and an hour later George W. Bush addressed the Texas Legislature (and the world) as president-elect. Indecision 2000 was over.

Analysis: Dimpled Chads and Dueling Courts

For the first several weeks after the election, the most debated questions were whether Gore was entitled to a manual recount by the canvassing boards, whether and how dimpled chads should be counted by the canvassing boards, and whether the time deadlines bound the canvassing boards. In the end these questions were moot, because, in the canvassing board counts, Bush led after every count and recount, regardless of what votes were counted, how they were counted or when they were counted. The story is in the duel between Scofla and Scotus in the contest proceedings.

Most Bush supporters vigorously attacked Scofla II as a deeply flawed, partisan decision by a Democrat court. Many Gore supporters, joined by constitutional scholars and media commentators, rose in furious response to Scotus II, contending that it was an ill-reasoned, illegitimate, politically motivated abuse of judicial power that would permanently damage Scotus. These charges are of enduring significance because they affect the reputation of the two courts and, in the case of the charges against Scotus, prompt many people to question the legitimacy of Bush's presidency. The best way to assess the charges against the two courts in to analyze Scofla II and Scotus II.

In ordering a statewide count of undervotes, Scofla exceeded its jurisdiction under Florida's election contest statute. The statute permits the contesting candidate to select the counties to be contested, and requires the canvassing boards of those counties to be joined in the contest action. This provision confines Scofla's jurisdiction and remedial power to the three counties that were parties to Gore's contest, depriving it of authority to order recounts in counties that were not joined in the action, which is of course what Scofla did.

Scofla also misapplies the provisions of the contest statute. The contest statute by its terms is designed to identify "legal votes" that were not counted by the county canvassing boards. Under Florida law, the canvassing boards can legally count votes by machine or by a hand count that counts *all* votes. Scofla ordered a hand count of *some* votes. Scofla thus counts votes that could not legally be counted by the canvassing board as "legal votes." This is absurd on the face of it, and is at odds with the provision requiring the canvassing boards to be made parties to the contest, for the obvious purpose of this requirement is to allow the canvassing boards to respond to charges that they had *wrongfully* failed to count votes.

Scofla's violations of the Florida election laws were critical. If Scofla had not illegally ordered a statewide count of undervotes, it would have upheld Judge Sauls, for it held that the selective count sought by Gore in his election contest was "inappropriate." If Scofla had followed the law, the election would have been over, and the Scotus involvement, with the *Sturm und Drang* that it caused, would not have occurred.

Scofla's violations of the contest statute were apparently unwitting—they are not mentioned in Scotus II or by the dissenters in Scofla II, so there is no reason to believe that the majority in Scofla II was aware of them. We cannot, however, forgive Scofla because it knew not what it did. Its obvious failure to follow the Florida contest statute violated Article II,

Section 1 of the United States Constitution, which requires the Florida electors to be appointed in the manner provided by Florida statutes.

Chalk up constitutional violation number one for Scofla.

Scofla II was decided late on December 8. It says that Florida has adopted the safe harbor provisions of 3 United States Code Section 5, requiring completion of all election contests by December 12. There were thus four days to rejigger the county computers to separate the undervotes from the other votes, select the public officials who would examine the undervotes, conduct this examination, allow the trial judge time to examine the reports of the examiners, consider objections to the decisions of the examiners and reach and render a decision, and allow Scofla time to hear and decide an appeal. There is no way this could be done consistent with the demands of procedural due process.

In Lindsey v. Normet[82] Scotus upheld the constitutionality of an Oregon statute allowing eviction of tenants for non-payment of rent. The statute called for a trial one week after the tenant was served with notice of the action, and it limited the defenses that could be used to avoid eviction. Asserting that a week was not enough time to prepare a defense, and that it was entitled to present all available defenses, the tenant claimed denial of procedural due process. Scotus denied the claim. Acknowledging that due process requires adequate time to prepare for trial, the Court said that a week was enough time in this case because the only issue was whether or not the rent had been paid. Acknowledging also that due process requires that a party be given an opportunity to assert his defenses, it upheld the limitation of defenses under the Oregon statute on the basis of established landlord-tenant law, and noted that damage claims based on other defenses could be pursued in a separate action.

Lindsey dealt with a statute that gave the parties a week to prepare for trial, placed no time limit on the presentation of the case or the conduct of an appeal, and involved a single, narrow issue. Scofla II dictated a procedure that allowed four days to prepare, present, contest, decide and appeal a case involving identification, counting and contesting of thousands of undervotes in 64 counties. There was no provision for a procedure or hearing to determine whether the evidence—the undervotes—was properly and fully identified. The evidence was to be examined, not by a trial judge or a person selected by him and subject to his control, but by scores of public officials scattered throughout the state who may or may not have experience in vote counts and procedures. Objections could not be made as "votes" were counted. There was no provision for, and realistically no time for, a trial court ballot-by-ballot hearing on contested ballots, which could have run in the thousands. There was no time to do anything in a thoughtful, orderly, judicious manner that assured a thorough, consistent examination of the ballots by competent, experienced examiners and allowed the parties to examine the evidence, assert their defenses and argue their case. The denial of procedural due process is obvious.

It is true that due process only requires what is possible under the circumstances. But even if Florida election law had permitted a statewide count of undervotes, it did not require it. As the dissenters noted in Scofla II, the majority voluntarily chose the impossible. Moreover, the time crunch was, for Gore and Scofla, a self-inflicted wound. Under Florida law, the judicial contest of the election cannot begin until the Florida election officials have certified the results from all of the counties. At Gore's request, Scofla delayed this certification for 10 days. Having run out the 24 second clock, Gore and Scofla can hardly complain that they had no time to shoot.

Chalk up constitutional violation number two for Scofla.

Scofla deliberately discriminated among voters. While purporting in Scofla II to order a statewide count of undervotes in the judicial contest, Scofla accepted the canvassing boards' manual recounts of undervotes in Broward, Palm Beach, Miami-Dade and Volusia counties. The standards in these recounts varied from county to county, and the standards changed during the counts in Palm Beach and Miami-Dade, so Scofla deliberately adopted an unequal treatment of voters, both between and within counties. When the count got underway on December 9 and it became apparent that the chaos and confusion of Scofla's electoral forced march was producing voting standards that varied from county to county and from counting table to counting table, Scofla denied Bush's motion to stay the count, deliberately accepting an unequal treatment of voters. And as the early returns of December 9 made clear, Scofla mandated a procedure that, with its lack of standards, press of time and use of scores of unsupervised, inexperienced vote counters, made variations in counting standards unavoidable. Scofla's repeated, deliberate denial of equal protection of the law is obvious.

The process for evaluating the undervotes violated procedural due process as well as equal protection. Scofla's hurry-up, use-the-janitors-if-you-have-to order for examining the undervotes was not only designed to examine ballots to determine votes in an election; it also established the method for evaluating the evidence in judicial proceedings—the election contest. Procedural due process does not permit a court to subject a body of evidence to varying and conflicting methods of evaluation.

Credit Scofla with a hat trick. It violated three constitutional provisions in a single opinion.

It appears that Scofla committed these constitutional infractions in service to a cause, for there is clear evidence of a partisan cast to Scofla's decisions. As noted, Scofla held in Scofla II that a count of undervotes in just a few counties was "inappropriate." The canvassing boards of Broward, Palm Beach, Miami-Dade and Volusia had conducted just such a count, and yet Scofla in Scofla I refused to stay this count and then bent the rules to accommodate it by giving an extra 12 days for the count to be completed. Why did Scofla I facilitate a count that was condemned by Scofla II? When Scofla I was under consideration, it was widely assumed that Scotus would not intervene, while review of Scofla II was almost inevitable. The conclusion is inescapable that Scofla was willing to facilitate an admittedly inappropriate, Gore-favoring count when it thought it could get by with it, but then retreated to the apparent safety of a statewide count when it knew that Scotus was looking over its shoulder.

There is further evidence that Scofla put its hand on the Gore side of the scale of justice. Scofla II purports to order a statewide judicial examination of all undervotes, but it accepted the 800 Gore votes that the canvassing boards in Broward, Palm Beach, Miami-Dade and Volusia counties had found in their examination of undervotes, and excluded these votes from the statewide recount that it ordered. This exclusion accepts a nonjudicial evaluation of ballots in a judicial contest, insulates the ballots from the scrutiny to which all other undervotes are subject, and deprives Bush of any opportunity to challenge these 800 votes. Scofla's acceptance of the undervotes found in the partial Miami-Dade manual recount is particularly egregious, for Florida law allows manual recounts only if all of the votes are hand-counted. Scofla thus accepts votes that were counted in an illegal partial recount as "legal votes." The shielding of Gore votes from the uncertainties of the judicial recount was too much even for Breyer and Souter, who said in Scotus II that a count of undervotes had to include *all* undervotes.

While ignoring Scofla's apparent president-making goal, Scotus' critics allege that the Scotus majority was driven by a consuming desire to deliver the presidency to George W. Bush. In *Supreme Injustice*, Professor Dershowitz launches a long, intemperate, groundless assault on the motives of the Scotus majority.[83] His "evidence" is nothing more than innuendo, alleged inconsistency with inapt prior decisions, and assumed Republican tendencies and personal motivations. For personal motivations, he speculates that Rehnquist and O'Connor were poised to retire, and wanted a Republican to pick their successors. Kennedy, he suggests, was angling to become Chief Justice. O'Connor and Rehnquist served for nearly five years after *Bush v. Gore*, with Rehnquist "retiring" only when he became the first justice to die in harness since his mentor Robert Jackson died of a heart attack in 1954. As for Kennedy's alleged attempt to become chief justice, Bush during the 2000 election had fingered Scalia and Thomas as his favorite justices, and had repeatedly criticized *Roe v. Wade*. As the justice who had provided the decisive vote to uphold *Roe*, Kennedy certainly knew that Bush would not move him to the Court's center chair. His chances might have been better under Gore.

Last I heard, Dershowitz had not apologized to Rehnquist, O'Connor and Kennedy.

If you're tired of reading about a court that broke the law and chose sides, relax. We come now to Scotus.

The commentators and academics characterize Scotus II as the product of a deeply divided court, but if we work through the opinions we find that, despite the contention and the occasional sound and fury, seven justices agreed that the standardless count ordered by Scofla II constituted a denial of equal protection of the law. The seven disagreed only on the deadline for resolving the dispute. The majority concluded that December 12 was the deadline because the Florida Legislature intended to take advantage of the safe harbor protection that federal law extended to electors who were not subject to challenge after December 12. Souter and Breyer claimed that the deadline was December 18, when the electors were to vote.

The deadline is a matter of Florida law, to be decided by Florida courts. David Boies, Gore's attorney, conceded in the oral arguments in Scofla I that the December 12 deadline applied, and both Scofla I and Scofla II held that this deadline applied. In Scofla I, Scofla said that election certifications could not be filed so late that they would "preclude Florida voters from participating fully in the federal electoral process." An accompanying footnote includes the safe harbor law as part of the "federal electoral process." In the "Applicable Law" discussion in Scofla II, Scofla quotes the safe harbor statute in full and states that the Florida presidential election statutes are "derived from" the safe harbor law. Later in the opinion, Scofla says that "because the selection and participation of Florida electors in the presidential election process is subject to a stringent calendar controlled by federal law, the Florida election law must yield" in the case of conflict with federal law. The December 12 safe harbor deadline is of course part of that "stringent calendar." (It is ironic and telling that the four justices who passionately insisted on deference to Scofla's construction of Florida law spurned Scofla's holding that December 12 was the deadline under Florida law. Souter and Breyer opted for December 18, while Stevens and Ginsburg said the contest could drag on until January 6.)

Even if the deadline was December 18, Souter and Breyer were wrong in concluding that the contest could be resolved by that date if the counting proceeded. The opinions in Scotus II were delivered late in the evening on December 12, so no Florida proceedings could have begun until December 13. Florida statutes required the Florida electors to meet in Tallahassee on December 18 and cast their votes at 10 a.m. Since the electors must get to Tallahassee from throughout the state, a final resolution of the contest would have had to be made by, say, noon on December 17. This leaves four days for a hearing to establish the counting standard, the conduct of the recount in 67 counties, a hearing to consider any disputed ballots, a decision by the trial court, an appeal to and decision by Scofla and, if necessary, an appeal to and decision by Scotus. Souter and Breyer admit that this is a "tall order," but it is more than that. It could not be done in any manner that satisfied the requirements of procedural due process.

Reading Scotus II, it is hard to see what the fuss is about. It is a well-reasoned case, solidly grounded in constitutional law. Scofla's denial of equal protection is obvious, and was recognized by nearly half of the Scofla judges and by seven of the Scotus judges, including two liberals (Souter and Breyer) and two moderates (O'Connor and Kennedy). Scofla decided the only state law issue involved (the contest deadline), so there is no question of poaching on state authority, as the dissenting justices and others contended. The deadline that forced Scotus to forbid further counting was acknowledged by Scofla itself.

The fact that the decision came when, as the majority said, the deadline was "upon us" was an accident of time caused by the tight time demands of the election laws and by Gore's decision to delay certification of the election, which robbed the judicial process of 10 of the 25 days that otherwise would have been available to contest the election. And far from being a "political" decision that exercised power entrusted to other branches of government, as many have charged, its resolution of a constitutional challenge discharged a duty clearly entrusted to the judiciary.

Scotus has been loudly and persistently criticized for taking the case, but the fact is that the Court would have been shirking its duty if it had not taken and resolved the case. The Florida Legislature was in the process of appointing presidential electors. If Scofla's count had handed the election to Gore, and Scotus had not intervened, Congress would have been presented with competing slates of electors when it met on January 6 to count the electoral votes. There would have been weeks of national angst, a donnybrook in an evenly-divided Congress, paralysis in the transition of power, and if congressional indecision or judicial intervention had delayed decision to or near January 20, a constitutional crisis. Seven justices agreed that Scofla's count was unconstitutional, and it would have been irresponsible for Scotus to stand aside while an unconstitutional vote count put the country through this wringer.

Scotus' stay of the Scofla II vote count has been criticized by academics and commentators. Shortly after Scotus II was decided, a raft of constutional law professors bought a full page in the *New York Times* to attack the stay. In view of the furor that would have erupted if Scofla's unconstitutional count had given Gore a temporary lead, it was reasonable for Scotus to preserve the status quo. The stay was in any event irrelevant, for with seven Scotus justices holding that a standardless count was unconstitutional, Scofla would have had to start over with a new count even if its original count had not been stayed. So no harm, no foul, as you would think at least some of the *New York Times* scholars would have realized, although it is probably hard to see the obvious when your gaze is diverted permanently to the left.

Scotus has been criticized for stepping into a political fray. In *Supreme Injustice*, Professor Dershowitz says that "courts ought not to jump into controversies that are political in nature."[84] But Scotus did not intervene in a political process; it intervened in a judicial process. The "votes" being counted as part of Scofla's two minute drill were not being counted pursuant to the political procedures for counting votes and determining a winner; they were evidence in a law suit. It is appropriate for a court with jurisdiction in the matter to review a decision of another court, as Scofla itself did when it reviewed Judge Saul's decision.

The decision in Scotus II could have been better. Ideally, it should have uncovered and condemned the full extent of Scofla's lawlessness, with a fuller explanation of its grounds for decision. But, faced with an out-of-control Scofla and the crush of time, it did the best it could. Unlike Scofla, it followed the law, and it ended what could have been a very dicey situation. It served the country well.

Count All Votes!

Many Democrats contend that, because some of the dimpled chads in Florida were not counted, George W. Bush is not a legitimate president. Several congressmen objected in the well of the United States Senate to Bush's 2000 election by the Electoral College. The always-ready-to-demagogue Jesse Jackson made the rounds of the talk shows asserting that Gore would be president if the dimpled chads had been counted, and President Clinton echoed this claim in a farewell tour during the waning days of his presidency.

Before the 2000 election, Florida had never counted any undervotes, let alone dimpled chads. In 1990, the Palm Beach County canvassing board adopted a policy that it would not count dimpled chads. Dimpled chad counting was not favored in Florida, and with good reason, for it does not produce an accurate count.

In a primary race for a congressional seat in Massachusetts, Philip Johnston emerged with a narrow victory. His opponent, William Delahunt, contested the election, asking for a recount of all votes, including dimpled chads. The trial court examined the dimpled chads, found that they contained enough votes to erase Johnston's margin, and declared Delahunt the victor. On appeal, the Massachusetts Supreme Court upheld the trial court and preserved Delahunt's victory, but it made its own examination of the dimpled chads and found that about three percent of the chads that the trial court included in its vote total were not, in fact, votes.[85] Thus, one nonpartisan counter in an unpartisan (primary) election found three percent more votes in the dimpled chads than another nonpartisan counter. Imagine how many more non-existent votes might be found in a general election count by canvassing boards who are no more detached than the chads.

The uncertainty in identifying chads indented enough to indicate a possible vote undermines the credibility of a dimpled chad count, but it is not the only, or even the most serious, difficulty in attempting to make the dimpled chads speak. A dimpled chad may be a vote, but it could also reflect a mistake realized or a mind changed or an abrasion caused by counting or handling the ballot. These alternatives may be unlikely, but it its also unlikely that a voter who clearly detached nine chads would dimple the tenth in an attempt to vote. The only explanation offered for the solitary dimple as a vote is the "chad build-up" theory that detached chads pile up in the voting machine beneath a candidate's name to the point that they impede the stylus. However, testimony before Judge Sauls indicated that it would take several elections to build such a pile, and that the chads drop to a recess at the end of the voting machine when it is upended for storage after each election. There is simply no way to force a dimpled chad to divulge its secret, so no such chad can be counted as a certain vote.

On the other hand, when the problem of the inscrutable chad is coupled with the uncertainty of identifying possible votes in the first place, we know with absolute certainty that a vote count based upon dimpled chads will be inaccurate, and that the more chads we count, the greater the error. And since dimpled chads will be counted only in close races, there will almost always be a possibility that the error in the count will exceed the margin of victory, handing the election to the real loser in the race. That was a distinct possibility in Florida, where the vote was so close that even a small inacurracy in the dimpled chad count could wrongfully deliver the election to Gore.

This is election by crapshoot. It does not count all votes, it is susceptible to partisan manipulation, it is not fair to the voters who properly cast their ballots, and it is not fair to the defeated candidate, as Mr. Johnston, the loser in the Massachusetts race, attested. In a column he wrote during the Florida contest, he discussed his experience. He is a Democrat, so the dimpled chad counting then going on favored his candidate, but he did not speak for a recount. On the contrary, while his words were measured, he obviously harbored a deep and abiding conviction that an errant process had cost him a seat in Congress.

The right to vote is a fundamental right, and a voter is entitled to have his or her vote counted if the vote is clear or can be determined with reasonable certainty. A voter who fails to follow simple and prominently displayed instructions is not entitled to have his uncertain vote counted by a process that can be manipulated, will produce an inaccurate count, and could well pick the wrong winner. The mistake in Florida lies not in failing to count all of the dimpled chads, but in counting any at all. George W. Bush was the legitimate winner in Florida.[86]

CHAPTER 6

The Nature of the Union —
Secession and States' Rights

In the late 1950s, San Antonio's privately owned mass transit system, like its counterparts in other major cities, was limping along, slowly losing its customers to urban sprawl and the automobile. The system was sold in 1959 to the City of San Antonio, which in 1978 sold it to the San Antonio Metropolitan Transit Authority, a public agency formed under a Texas law providing for countywide mass transit authorities.

As we saw in Chapter 2, the Supreme Court in the 1941 *Darby* case upheld the Fair Labor Standards Act as a legitimate exercise of congressional power under the interstate commerce clause. In 1959, when San Antonio bought the transit system, the wage and hour provisions of the act did not apply to state and local government employees. In 1966, however, the act was extended to most public transit workers, and in 1974 it was extended to nearly all state and local government workers. In 1979, the Department of Labor issued regulations subjecting the San Antonio Metropolitan Transit Authority to the act.

The authority resisted the regulation, and it probably thought its case was a slam dunk. In *National League of Cities v. Usery*, the Supreme Court had recently held that it was unconstitutional to apply the wage and hour provisions of the act to public employees performing "traditional government functions."[87] Based upon a history of publicly owned and operated mass transit in the United States, the authority was confident that mass transit was a traditional government function, so with a nine year old precedent in its corner the authority no doubt expected vindication when the Supreme Court rendered its decision in *Garcia v. San Antonio Metropolitan Transit Authority*.[88]

The authority was in for a rude awakening, learning that the Supreme Court followed precedent only when it wanted to. In an opinion authored by a flip-flopping Harry Blackmun of *Roe v. Wade* fame, who had been in the *Usery* majority, a 5-4 majority of the Supreme Court scrapped the "traditional government function" line of cases, specifically overruled *Usery*, and held that Congress had pretty much free reign to apply the commerce clause to the states.

Four justices dissented. Noting that a number of the majority justices had repeatedly voiced support for *Usery* during its brief lifetime, the dissenters said that a state's sovereignty insulated its government functions from federal control.

Garcia is wrong, but not only for the reason advanced by its dissenters.

States are of course sovereign. The federal government must respect that sovereignty, and may not exert federal power in a manner that impedes the states' ability to perform their "traditional government functions." But the states' immunity from federal power is broader than this. It is the nature of the federal government, not just the states' sovereign status, that limits federal power over the states. The states are not subjects of the federal government, so the federal government has no more authority over the states than it has over the government of France or the residents of Fiji, except as specifically set forth in the Constitution. Whether or not the states are performing "traditional government functions," they are not subject to the jurisdiction of the United States.

To determine the nature of the federal government, and confirm that the states are not subject to its jurisdiction, we will discuss the "right" of secession. It is an asserted right grounded in a vision of the federal union, and we fought the Civil War over it, so the discussion will inform the present and illuminate the past.

The "Right" of Secession

In a 2001 article in *North & South* magazine, Kent Masterson Brown, echoing ante-bellum Southern leaders like Jefferson Davis and John C. Calhoun, argues that the Constitution permits secession by individual states.[89] He supports his conclusion largely by quoting statements by Founders and other political thinkers that characterize the Union as a "compact" among the states, with little analysis of the provisions of the Constitution or examination of the government that it created, and no discussion of secession's impact. In determining whether the Constitution authorizes secession, it is not enough to pin a label on the document.[90] We must consider the nature of the government that it created, analyze its provisions and assess the consequences of secession for the citizens of the seceding state.

The Nature of the Union

As the name suggests, the United States is undeniably a union of states. Article VII of the Constitution provides that ratification by the conventions of nine states shall establish the

Constitution "between the states so ratifying the same." Article IV, Section 3 empowers Congress to admit "new states...into this Union."

But what is the nature of this union? Is it a compact among the states—another partnership, like the union created by the Articles of Confederation—as Brown contends. Or does the union simply set the geographical bounds of a separately established, direct-acting, fully sovereign government of the American people independent of and beyond control of the states—a government which, in the words of Gouverneur Morris, the Constitution's draftsman, has a "complete and compulsive operation"?[91] The best way to answer these questions is to consider the government established by the Constitution.

The government established by the Constitution has no attributes of partnership. The states are rarely mentioned, they never meet to exercise control over their "compact," and they have no right of control. As discussed below, the states do not even retain power to amend the Constitution. The only powers the states have are the powers to elect senators and to establish the method of appointing presidential electors.

There is, on the other hand, abundant evidence in the Constitution that it creates a sovereign national government of the people, independent of the states. Congress is empowered without consent of the states to, among other things, lay taxes directly on its citizens, raise troops and regulate commerce among the states. It laws "shall be the supreme law of the land...anything in the constitution or laws of any state to the contrary notwithstanding." Congress, and not the states, is authorized to admit new states to the Union. It is a strange "partnership" in which the partnership does not act through the partners, has power which is beyond the partners' control, and can admit new partners without the consent of any existing partners. Except for the big state-small state compromise embodied in the composition of the Senate, representation in Congress and election of the president is by population rather than by state.[92]

To return to the questions we began with, the government created by the Constitution is clearly a fully sovereign government of the American people beyond the control of the states, and not a compact of the states.

The Terms of the Constitution

There are a number of provisions of the Constitution that are inconsistent with both a compact theory of the states and a right of secession.

The preamble of the Constitution states that "We the people of the United States…do ordain and establish this Constitution for the United States of America." Lincoln and others have argued that this language confirms that the Union is a government of people and not of states. Brown counters by alleging that the reference here is to the people of the individual states rather than to the people of the United States as a whole. He may be right, but it is hard to see what difference it makes. People of a state are clearly distinct from the state as a sovereign, and the people of all of the states taken together are the people of the United States.

The Constitution addresses creation[93] and expansion[94] of the Union and amendment of the Constitution. It is unlikely that delegates who provided for formation and growth of the Union and change in its charter would have contemplated or condoned a power to dissolve the Union without providing for it, particularly since dissolution involves the obvious issues of allocation and disposition of national obligations and assets. State partnership statutes, drafted presumably by thinkers less profound and far-sighted than the Founders, routinely include provisions for settling obligations and disposing of assets if the venture is dissolved. In the context of a document which addresses the essential attributes of the Union, the absence of a stated right of secession is the dog that didn't bark.

Another silent dog lurks in the amendment power. Article V of the Constitution says that amendments may be proposed by a vote of two thirds of both houses of Congress or by a convention called by Congress on application of two thirds of the states, and can be ratified by the legislatures of three fourths of the states or by conventions in three fourths of the states, "as the one or the other mode of ratification may be proposed by Congress." A close reading of this provision discloses that no state or combination of states has the power to propose amendments, and no power to ratify an amendment unless Congress refers the proposed amendment to state legislatures rather than state conventions. In other words, the states, even if acting unanimously, do not have power to amend the Constitution. The state legislatures acting unanimously could not amend the Constitution to dissolve the Union, so what gives a single state legislature the power to dismember the Union at will by seceding from the Union?

Article VI of the Constitution states that "the members of the several state legislatures...shall be bound by oath or affirmation, to support this Constitution." Secession can only be voted by the state legislatures or by conventions called by them, and legislation is obviously necessary to make secession effective. Proponents of a right of secession could argue that secession is not incompatible with this provision since, if a right of secession exists under the Constitution, a legislature that votes secession does not violate its oath of fealty to the Constitution. However, this provision applies not only to state legislators, but also to all senators and congressman and all executive and judicial officers of the United States, so in context the required fealty is fealty within the Union, which is incompatible with a vote for or support of secession. And the demand that the pledge of allegiance come from state legislators rather than the states confirms that the Union is a government of the people and not the states, both because the states are excluded and because the demand suggests that the legislators swear allegiance as both state officials and American citizens.

The Impact of Secession

If the right of secession exists, it could be voted at any time by a simple majority of the legislature, and it would deprive the citizens of the seceding state of their United States citizenship. They would lose the right to travel abroad and among the states. They would lose the benefits of the full faith and credit, privilege and immunities and interstate commerce clauses of the Constitution. They would lose the protection of the United States armed forces and the status and intangible benefits that United States membership confers. They would become subject in an unsettled way to liability for national obligations for which the seceding state is liable.

The nature of national citizenship is such that a state cannot deprive its citizens of United States citizenship. It is a citizenship that is conferred by the Constitution or federal law, and cannot be destroyed by another sovereign. A state could not, for example, deprive a person of United States citizenship as a penalty for murder or other crimes. There is no reason to assume that an implied right of secession is an exception to this general rule.

On the contrary, the amending provisions give strong testimony that the Constitution protects rights of national citizenship from state action. As we have seen, state legislatures cannot propose constitutional amendments, and they can ratify amendments only if Congress gives them the power to do so. The government created by the Constitution is the people's government, ordained and established by "the people of the United States." The amending provisions assure that the states cannot deprive the people of the benefits of their government, which is of course what secession would do.

The Significance of the Secession Debate

The debate over the right of secession had practical significance in 1860. The claimed legality of secession no doubt gave it support in the Southern states and legitimacy abroad and even in the North which it would not have enjoyed if it had been recognized as rebellion or revolution. Southerners who characterized the Civil War as The War Between the States or The War of Northern Aggression would presumably be less comfortable with The War of Southern Revolution. But in the absence of a persuasive case for a right of secession, that's what it was.

The Pernicious Abstraction

Until late in the Civil War, Lincoln consistently rejected secession as an act without legal effect.[95] Yet when asked in a reconstruction context whether the states were in or out of the Union, he dismissed the question as a "pernicious abstraction."[96] During congressional Reconstruction most

Northern radicals, though driven generally by spite and vindictiveness, did not press the Johnson or Grant administrations to try the Confederate leaders for treason or other crimes.[97] Why in the reconstruction context was Lincoln coy on secession, and the radicals reluctant to try the "traitors"? Probably because they did not want the courts to determine the legality of secession. If secession was unconstitutional, the seceding states remained in the Union, and could not have been treated as though they were out of the Union, which is, in fact, how the North treated them. West Virginia, which was carved out of Virginia during the war, could not legally be admitted as a state because of the constitutional provision that a state cannot be carved out of another state without its consent.[98] Congress could not constitutionally refuse to seat congressional delegations from the seceded states, as it did during Reconstruction. The president and Congress could not constitutionally establish qualifications for voters in the seceding states, as they did before and during Reconstruction. Congress could not constitutionally require the seceding states to ratify the Fourteenth Amendment as a condition to readmission as states, as it did during Reconstruction. It could not constitutionally subject the seceding states to military government, as it did during Reconstruction.[99] Thus the North had good reason to avoid a judicial decision on the right of secession.[100]

Why Lincoln's Union Limits
Federal Power Over the States

It is generally assumed that the compact theory of the Union favors states' rights, while Lincoln's vision of an indissoluble union favors federal power over the states. In all things save a right of secession, exactly the opposite is true.

Our exploration of the nature of the federal government and the terms of the Constitution vindicates Lincoln. As he said, the government of the United States is, under the Constitution, a government of the "people of the United States," as expressed in the Constitution's Preamble. It is not a compact of states, but a sovereign government of the people, by the people, for the people, as Lincoln said in the Gettysburg address, created and existing independent of the states. Its subjects are the people of the United States—American citizens and those, such as immigrants and visitors, who have subjected themselves to American jurisdiction by residing in this country. The states are *not* subjects of the federal government. In *McCulloch v. Maryland*, Chief Justice Marshall confirmed that a government can only operate upon, and only has jurisdiction over, its subjects.

In *McCulloch*, Maryland had taxed the Second Bank of the United States, a federal instrumentality. After concluding that a bank was a legitimate means of implementing federal power, Marshall considered the constitutionality of the Maryland tax. He struck it down. In the course of his opinion, he rejected the suggestion that Maryland could tax the bank because it was physically located in Maryland. "All subjects over which a sovereign power of a state extends," he said, "are objects of taxation; but those over which it does not extend are exempt from taxation."[101] Since the federal government was not a subject of the state of Maryland, Maryland could not tax it. Marshall was speaking of taxes, but the principle also applies to other powers. It has been held, for example, that the states cannot subject federal buildings to state building codes. And just as the federal government is not a subject of the states, the states are not subjects of the federal government, so, except as specifically provided in the Constitution, the federal government has no more power over the states than the states have over the federal government.[102]

The Constitution limits state power in a number of respects. Under Article I, Section 10, the states cannot, among other things, enter into treaties, coin money, impair contracts, pass ex post facto laws, grant titles of nobility, or levy taxes on imports or exports. And as we have seen, under the interstate commerce clause the states cannot exert their power in a way that disrupts or discriminates against interstate or foreign commerce.

While the Constitution restricts state power, there is nothing in the Constitution to suggest that the states can be subjected to federal power as though they were citizens of the United States. On the contrary, the first listed congressional power in Article I, Section 8 of the Constitution is the power to "levy and collect taxes." It is fanciful to assume that this provision permits taxation of the states, as opposed to the "people of the United States," and there is no indication that other powers are designed to permit Congress to treat states as though they were citizens. It is this lack of federal power over the states, as well as the sovereignty of the states, that deprives Congress of the power to subject states to the wage and hour provisions of the Fair Labor Standard Act or to any other federal statutes of general applicability. As in so many other areas that we have explored in this book, the Supreme Court must revisit its decisions expanding federal control over the states, and return to the Constitution.

The Constitution to return to is arguably not the one in the books, which contains amendments of dubious constitutionality. The Constitution permits amendment of its terms, but a constitution can ordinarily only be amended to alter the relationship between a government and its citizens—the Constitution could not be amended to impose its terms on the government of France or the citizens of Fiji. Several of the post-Civil War amendments of the Constitution, including the Fourteenth, which contains the due process clause, and the Fifteenth, Nineteenth and Twenty-Sixth, which deprive the states of power to deny the right to vote based on race, sex or the age of anyone over 17, restrict state power and give the federal government power over the states to enforce the restrictions. Since these amendments impose their will on states that are not subjects of the federal government, they would appear to be unconstitutional. The Supreme Court, however, would *never* reach this conclusion. It could uphold the amendments in question by deciding that the states, in consenting to a Constitution that permitted amendments and imposed restrictions on state power, implicitly agreed to further amendments restricting state power, with the federal government empowered to enforce those restrictions.

CHAPTER 7

Grab Bag of Constitutional Shenanigans

In earlier chapters we have discovered how courts have misread and defiled the Constitution in several major areas. In this chapter we will explore four more constitutional miscreants—the Supreme Court's misuse of the due process clause in its decisions addressing the death penalty and the privilege against self-incrimination, its misreading of the equal protection clause and the Civil Rights Act of 1964 in the Michigan reverse discrimination case, and the Democrats' Constitution-defying use of the filibuster to block confirmation of presidential nominees.

Death Penalty Cases—Ideology Swamps Reason

The Supreme Court's line of cases restricting the death penalty did not have a good debut in its 1972 rollout.

The year before the debut, the Supreme Court, in *McGautha v. California*, had considered the constitutionality of death penalty statutes in California and Ohio.[103] Earlier, the Court had used the incorporation doctrine to apply the Eighth Amendment's ban on cruel and unusual punishment to the states, and had employed the ban to strike down punishments if their nature or severity offended "evolving standards of decency." The laws of California and Ohio, like the laws of most states, left it up to the uncontrolled discretion of the jury to decide whether convicted murderers should live or die. The defendants argued that the jury's standardless punishment discretion was unconstitutional.

The Supreme Court rejected the argument. The Court noted that standardless sentencing statutes had been adopted by many states, observed that they had been repeatedly challenged without success in state and federal appellate courts, and said that, with this background, "it requires a strong showing to upset this settled practice of the Nation on constitutional grounds." Then, after explaining that experience with sentencing standards disclosed that they provided no more certainty than jury discretion, the Court held that "in light of history, experience and the present limitation of human knowledge, we find it impossible to say that committing to the untrammeled discretion of the jury the power of life or death in capital cases is offensive to anything in the Constitution."

Little did *McGautha* know that, within a year, it would be killed and buried in an unmarked grave.

In *Furman v Georgia*, the Supreme Court overturned death sentences in Georgia for murder and rape, and a death sentence in Texas for rape.[104] In a 10 line, 5-4 "Per Curiam" opinion, signed by no judge and setting forth no reasons, the Court held that the sentences constituted cruel and unusual punishments.

Many of the justices wrote opinions. Two of the majority justices—Thurgood Marshall and William Brennan—believed that the death penalty was unconstitutional in all cases, ignoring the Fifth and Fourteenth Amendment provisions acknowledging that the federal and state governments can take life with due process of law. The other three majority justices—William Douglas, Byron White and Potter Stewart—voted to strike down the statutes because they gave juries unbridled sentencing discretion. Thus the deciding votes on the Court, and the effect of the decision, overruled the thorough, well-reasoned *McGautha* decision that had been decided a year earlier and had confirmed a long string of state and federal cases upholding standardless punishment statutes.

Furman did not do the Supreme Court proud. It struck down the death penalty laws of nearly all of the states in a 10 line, unsigned, unreasoned opinion that overruled a year old precedent without fessing up to what it was doing. But *Furman* was just the beginning; things would get worse.

In response to *Furman*'s holding that standardless death penalty statutes were unconsititutional, a number of states passed statutes imposing a clear standard by requiring the death penalty in all cases for specified crimes. Can't do that, the Supreme Court held in a 5-4 decision in *Woodson v. North Carolina*.[105] Automatic death penalty statutes, it held, offended "evolving standards of decency." As evidence of widespread opposition to automatic death penalties, the Court cited alleged refusal of juries to convict guilty defendants under automatic death statutes and the action of state legislatures that responded to this jury nullification by enacting statutes giving juries discretion to elect life imprisonment or death. In his dissent, Justice Rehnquist pointed out that these two examples of public sentiment were really only one, for the majority admitted that the legislatures acted only because nullifying juries forced their hands. Thus, says Rehnquist, "evolving standards of decency" are evidenced by nothing more than the assumed but unknowable actions of an unknown number of juries.

In *Woodson*, North Carolina contended that the automatic death penalty statutes enacted in response to *Furman* were themselves evidence of "evolving standards of decency." The Court majority admitted that a "number of states"—it carefully avoided saying how many—had enacted automatic death penalty statutes, but denied that they evidenced the required standards of decency. So a Court that had just cited legislative response to nullifying juries as compelling evidence of evolving decency standards now denied that legislative response to *Furman* provided evidence of such standards. The Court should have heeded Clarence Darrow's advice against acting with unseemly haste. Darrow said he once turned down a potential client who promised to obtain Darrow's fees quickly by observing that his fees could not be paid with money that had been stolen—and here he paused for effect—"so recently."

Furman and *Woodson*, by rejecting both standardless sentencing and automatic death penalties, require standards to guide the life and death decision. The standard that has evolved is a balancing of "mitigating" and "aggravating" factors that, in the words of *Woodson*, "accords..significance to relevant facets of the character and record of the individual offender and the circumstances of the particular offense." The question then became whether judge or jury evaluates the mitigating and aggravating factors and chooses life or death.

From time immemorial, judges have made sentencing decisions within punishment ranges specified by the legislature. Say, for example, that a statute dictates imprisonment of from 10 to 25 years for armed robbery. Following a jury's guilty verdict, the court holds a sentencing hearing, considers whatever it thinks appropriate, and imposes a sentence within the prescribed range. Based upon this practice, the Supreme Court held in *Walton v Arizona*[106] and a number of other cases that a judge could in death sentence cases receive evidence of mitigating and aggravating factors, balance the two, and impose sentence.

In *Ring v. Arizona* the Court reversed *Walton* and its other cases.[107] Since a court's finding of aggravating factors could result in a sentence—the death penalty—not permitted on the basis of the jury's verdict, the Court said, these factors were an element of the crime that had to be presented to the jury.

Ring is illogical and at odds with the long-established sentencing practices described above. Like a statute setting a 10-25 year range for armed robbery, Arizona's death penalty statute specified a range of punishment—life imprisonment or death. And like a judge imposing a death sentence based upon aggravating factors presented to the judge, a judge sentencing the robber to the maximum 25 year sentence presumably does so by considering matters not presented to the jury.

The Supreme Court's decisions limiting those eligible for execution have been as mindless and changeable as its other death penalty decisions.

In *Penry v. Lynaugh*, decided in 1989, the Supreme Court allowed execution of a person with mild mental retardation.[108] It noted that there were various degrees of retardation and that 35 of the 37 death penalty states allowed execution of the mentally retarded, and it held that judges and juries must weigh mental retardation as a mitigating factor in making the life or death decision. Thirteen years later, in *Atkins v. Virginia*, the Court overruled itself, categorically banning execution of the mentally retarded regardless of the degree of retardation.[109] It said that, during that 13 year span, "evolving standards of decency" had shifted against execution of the retarded, citing as evidence the facts that execution of the retarded was not permitted in 30 of the 50 states, including 12 that had banned the death penalty altogether, that several states had banned such executions since *Penry* was decided, and that the "world community" was unalterably opposed to execution of the retarded. Reversing the position taken in earlier cases, the Court also said that it could bring its own judgment to bear on the acceptability of the death penalty, and it agreed with the 30 states and the world community.

The Supreme Court's juvenile execution decisions follow the path of the decisions addressing execution of the mentally retarded. In *Stanford v. Kentucky*, the Court allowed execution of 16 and 17 year olds, noting that 22 of 37 death penalty states permitted execution of minors over 15.[110] The widespread acceptance of juvenile execution by death penalty states, the Court said, belied any "evolving standard of decency" against juvenile executions. Sixteen years later, in *Roper v. Simmons*, the Court overruled itself.[111] Stating, as it had in *Atkins*, that 30 of the 50 states did not allow execution of juveniles, that the "world community" had set its face against these executions, and that the majority justices themselves didn't much like them, the Court said that standards of decency had evolved to the point that execution of juveniles was no longer permitted.

Justice Scalia dissented in both *Atkins* and *Roper*. His opinions are forceful, compelling and devastating; a column in the liberal *Washington Post* concedes that Kennedy's majority opinion in *Roper* cannot withstand Scalia's dissenting opinion. Neatly capturing his objection to the proposition that American standards of justice can be found in world opinion and the personal values of individual justices, he said that "because I do not believe that the meaning of the Eighth Amendment...should be determined by five members of this Court or like-minded foreigners, I dissent." He pointed out that the majority used statistical sleight of hand by claiming that 30 of 50 states did not permit execution of juveniles and the mentally retarded. Twelve of the 30 do not have the death penalty, and there is of course no way of knowing whether they would permit execution of juveniles or the retarded if they were to enact the death penalty. Indeed, while Scalia does not say so, the absence of the death penalty in a state is not even evidence of widespread opposition to the death penalty in that state; it could as readily reflect inertia or an inclination to leave well enough alone. Twenty of the 38 death penalty states, a clear majority, allowed execution of 16 and 17 year olds and the mentally retarded.

In *Roper*, neither the majority nor the minority opinions mentioned *Planned Parenthood of Central Mo. v. Danforth*,[112] but they should have. In *Roper*, Kennedy says that 16 and 17 year olds are not fully mature, unable to fully appreciate the gravity and consequences of their acts. Yet in *Danforth* the Court held that any girl old enough to get pregnant has a constitutional right to decide whether to bear or kill the life within. So five justices of the Supreme Court, with a self-proclaimed right to impose their personal death penalty values on the rest of us, decide that a girl of tender years is competent to determine whether another being will live or die, while a street wise 17 going on 40 juvenile is not mature enough to comprehend the stigma and penalties that society attaches to calculated, cold-blooded, first degree murder. Go figure.

The majority opinion in *Roper v. Simmons* ignores the question of timing. *Stanford* was decided in 1989, *Roper*, which overruled it, in 2005. The *Roper* majority opinion carefully avoids telling us when Simmons' crime was committed, but the Missouri Supreme Court opinion in the case informs us that Simmons murdered his victim in 1993, much closer in time to *Stanford* than to *Roper*. In assessing punishment, why not look to community standards when the crime is committed? Why should a criminal be allowed to escape justice by gaming the system for a decade and more? In his dissent in *Atkins*, Scalia notes that 11 of the 18 states that banned execution of the mentally retarded did not apply the ban to crimes committed or convictions obtained before the ban.

The Supreme Court decisions limiting the death penalty are a disgrace. They are poorly-reasoned and emotion-driven, cook the statistical books, reject American conceptions of suitable punishment in favor of world opinion and the personal values of a court majority, and mock the Court's claimed attachment to precedent, flip-flopping more often and more quickly than a fish out of water. The Court adopted and then quickly reversed its positions on standardless punishment decisions, judicial sentencing, execution of the mentally retarded, execution of juveniles, and the power of the Court to determine "evolving standards of decency" without supporting evidence. The Court reminds one of Captain Braxton Bragg of the United States Army, later Lieutenant General Bragg of the Confederate Army. Bragg was an ill-tempered martinet who constantly bickered with his fellow officers. Once, as officer of the day, he reported himself for a number of infractions. Responding to the report, Bragg's exasperated commanding officer said "Bragg, you have quarreled with every other officer in this command, and now you are quarreling with yourself."

Racial Preferences—Heavy Hand on the Scales of Justice

At the end of its 2002-2003 term, the Supreme Court delivered two 5-4 decisions responding to challenges to the University of Michigan's penchant for racial and ethnic preferences. In *Gratz v. Bollinger*,[113] it struck down the undergraduate admissions process as a thinly-disguised quota system. In *Grutter v. Bollinger*, it upheld the law school's more sophisticated means of achieving racial and ethnic balance.[114] We deal here with *Grutter*.

The *Grutter* majority opinion opens by summarizing the Supreme Court's prior reaction to race-based discrimination. In applying the equal protection clause, the Court said, it has upheld racially discriminatory laws only if they survive "strict scrutiny" by the Court, advance a "compelling state interest," and employ the narrowest possible means of achieving their objectives.

The Court then turns to the law school's admission program, beginning with the school's explanation of and justification for its group preferences. The school considers race and ethnicity in selecting its students, to be sure, but these are but two of a host of things evaluated in the admissions process. Once in a while, a rejected minority applicant has better college and LSAT scores than accepted white applicants. The school does seek a "critical mass" of minority students, which might smack of a quota, but this is simply a way of determining that its program is working. The goal of the program is to "achieve that diversity which has the potential to enrich everyone's education," and to assure that no minority group will "feel isolated" within the law school community. The school enlists a host of prominent public and corporate supporters who testify that a diverse school mix is needed to achieve a diverse work force.

The *Grutter* majority buys it. The school's admission process receives passing grades in the "strict scrutiny," "compelling state interest," and "narrowly tailored means" tests.

The four dissenters, each with a separate opinion, will have none of it. What the school sells as a broad-based attempt to achieve diversity, they say, is nothing but a disguised program to favor African-Americans. In response to the school's claim that it protects various minority groups from feeling isolated, the dissenters note that in a typical year the school accepts about 100 Blacks, 50 Hispanics and 15 Native Americans. How is it that Blacks need 100 of their fellows to avoid a sense of isolation, while Hispanics can get by with half as many and American Indians find comfort in a relative handful?

The dissenters observe that academic standards vary widely from one protected group to another. In the 2000 applicant pool, all of the Black applicants with grade point averages of 3.0 or more and LSAT scores of 159-160 were admitted, while only about one-sixth of Hispanics with comparable scores were. Drop the LSAT score to 151-153, and 60 percent of Blacks are admitted while only six percent of Hispanics make the cut. While the dissents do not look at the scores of White applicants, it seems likely that the White applicant success ratio at these levels of academic performance is lower than Hispanics.

The dissenters look at the small handful of rejected minority applicants who scored better than accepted White applicants. Nearly all of them were Hispanic.

The dissenters believe that the system is, in fact, a quota system. The "critical mass" approach suggests as much, and the fact that the percentage of accepted minority members varies little from year to year bears further evidence of a quota. Most tellingly, while the school claims that it puts only a light minority-favoring thumb on the scales of admissions justice, that thumb is replaced with a heavy hand in the end stages of the process. Then, the admissions officers get daily tracking reports of minority admissions, and they are authorized to further lower the standards if needed to achieve critical mass.

The dissenters deny that "diversity" or anything like it has ever before been used to override the equal protection clause. They also deny that Michigan's diversity program is the narrowest possible response to a minority admissions shortfall. Michigan's law school is one of the best in the country, with highly selective admission standards that disproportionately exclude minority applicants. Michigan pursues a minority-excluding course, and then tries to sweeten its bitter fruit by discriminating against White and, to a lesser extent, Hispanic applicants. The narrowest and best response to the minority admission problem, the dissenters say, is to reduce admission standards, making changes in the school as the Virginia Military Institute was required to do when the Supreme Court forced it to admit women.

Analytically, the *Grutter* dissenters clearly make the better case than the majority. Even they, however, ignore an important stranger at the table.

Both the majority and minority opinions acknowledge that the Michigan admissions programs invoke not only the equal protection clause, but also 42 United States Code section 2000d, part of the Civil Rights Act of 1964. The opinions introduce this provision, but they don't discuss it, assuming, apparently, that it simply mirrors the equal protection clause. It is much broader than the equal protection clause, its ban on racial and ethnic discrimination categorical and unconditional.

Section 2000d says that "no person shall, on the ground of race...be subjected to discrimination under any program or activity receiving Federal financial assistance." This provision proves once again that the United States Code has every tax but syntax, but the point is clear. Its ban on discrimination is a categorical imperative, as stark and unyielding as the commandments the Supreme Court so recently tossed from the Nation's courthouses. There is no hint here of "strict scrutiny" or "compelling state interests" or "narrowly tailored" solutions. This is the kind of language Senator Humphrey had in mind when he assured skeptics that he would eat the pages of the Civil Rights Act if it was read to permit reverse discrimination. There may be some flexibility in the concept of "equal protection," but there is none in section 2000d's edict against race-based discrimination. Such discrimination is prohibited, clearly and in no uncertain terms. And it clearly occurs in the Michigan admissions program, which is a zero sum game. Each year, Michigan's law school has about 350 in its entering class, so any accepted minority applicant closes the door to a majority applicant. And yet none of the justices, in either case or on either side, engages this statute in any meaningful way.

Supporters often use geographical and cultural preferences to justify racial and ethnic preferences. It is true that many college and post-graduate programs use geography and cultural background to evaluate applicants, but these preferences differ in kind from racial and ethnic preferences. It is unlikely that applicants admitted on the basis of geography and culture fall within a constant, predictable range year after year; barely possible that they have performance scores at or below the scores of successful racial and ethnic applicants; and inconceivable that they are the obsessive objects of daily tracking reports in the last stages of the admissions process, with standards relaxed to achieve a "critical mass."

Michigan's widespread support from government and business groups is predictable, and means little. They are encouraged by the law and compelled by their culture to achieve a diverse work force, and a hard and fast rule against racial and ethnic discrimination might upset their diversity applecarts and subject them to an increased risk of liability.

The use of "diversity" to override constitutional and statutory commands does not hold water, as we can see if we test it for leaks.

It is 2020. Michigan's program of racial and ethnic preferences, and similar programs elsewhere, have been successful, dramatically increasing minority enrollment. Meanwhile, as they have done for 20 years or more, women continue to outperform men at all levels of education, producing a disproportionate percentage of women in graduate and post-graduate programs, and they tend to perform better than men. Studies and anecdotal evidence suggest that white men are becoming the least-favored group in government and the private sector, as employers choose minority applicants for balance and women for success. As a result of all this, white males on campus feel beleaguered, and it adversely affects their academic performance and campus culture. Voucher programs and long-standing Republican control of the United States Department of Education have raised minority performance in primary and secondary schools, reducing the need for minority preferences. A number of experts confirm that elimination of these preferences will help minority students, giving them the confidence that comes from making it on their own. These same experts determine that an increase in the male to female ratio would be good for everybody. Michigan weighs all of these factors, and elects to modify its admissions program to give a thumb-on-the-scale preference to white males, and to keep the thumb there and increase the pressure until a "critical mass" is achieved. Minority and women's groups challenge the Michigan program. We all know who would win.

The Privilege Against Self-Incrimination—
A Right in Search of a Rationale

The Fifth Amendment states that no person "shall be compelled in any criminal case to be a witness against himself." Anyone who says he knows why this privilege against self-incrimination deserves constitutional protection has not thought about the matter very much.

The privilege is not needed to reject confessions involuntarily extracted by physical abuse or third degree interrogation methods; they would be excluded from trial by the demands of procedural due process and the refusal of courts to admit non-credible evidence. The real function of the privilege is to allow accused criminals to refuse to testify in open court or other public venue, under no threat of physical or mental abuse other than the risk of imprisonment for contempt of court if they refuse to testify or for perjury if they give false testimony. Why, as a matter of fundamental fairness or constitutional right, should an accused criminal be treated differently from any other witness?

For a long time, the Supreme Court held that the privilege against self-incrimination was not rooted in the demands of fundamental justice. In *Twining v. New Jersey*, decided in 1908, the Court held that procedural due process under the Fourteenth Amendment did not require the states to observe the privilege against self-incrimination. In a concise, well-reasoned opinion, Justice William Moody explored the historical origins and development and then-current status of the privilege. The privilege is not found in the Magna Carta, he said, and did not apply in English law for several hundred years after the Magna Carta was issued in 1215. While many ratifying states requested a Bill of Rights when they ratified the

Constitution, only a handful included the privilege against self-incrimination in their proposed catalog of protected rights. When the Constitution was adopted, many states did not recognize the privilege, and even in 1908 it was not observed in civilized non-English speaking countries. In summary, he said that "the wisdom of the [privilege] has never been universally assented to…many doubt it today, and it is best defended not as an unchangeable of universal justice, but as a law proved by experience to be expedient…It has no place in the jurisprudence of civilized and free countries outside the domain of the common law."[115] With this background, Moody had no trouble concluding that the states could forgo the privilege against self-incrimination if they wanted to.

Unlike many other Supreme Court decisions from the early 1900s, *Twining* was not rejected as the ranting of a reactionary court when the liberals achieved power. On the contrary, liberals embraced it. In 1937, Justice Cardozo, a liberal icon, cited it with enthusiastic approval,[116] and in 1947 the Roosevelt Court affirmed it, with Frankfurter in a concurring opinion stating that Moody's *Twining* opinion was among the Supreme Court's greatest opinions.[117]

Twining's honeymoon ended in 1964, when the Supreme Court held that the incorporation doctrine applied the privilege against self-incrimination to the states.[118] In 1965, the Court held that a state trial judge violated the privilege when he told the jury that it could draw conclusions from the defendant's failure to testify.[119] The next year, in *Miranda v. Arizona*, a 5-4 majority of the Court conferred mystical status on this recently pooh-poohed privilege, and held that the privilege required a pre-questioning statement to suspects advising them that they didn't have to talk if they didn't want to and that anything they said could be used against them—the now-famous Miranda warning.[120] Justices

Harlan and White wrote dissenting opinions, pointing out that the Court had consistently and repeatedly refused to require pre-questioning warnings to suspects, and that the majority had used vague, unsubstantiated fears of police abuse to dictate interrogation procedures for the entire country.

My purpose here is not to attack the privilege against self-incrimination. The Fifth Amendment applies it to the federal government, and it is included in the constitutions of most if not all states. Even states not constitutionally required to apply it might adopt it on prudential grounds, feeling that criminal defendants forced to testify would probably lie, and that it would be a waste of prosecutorial and judicial resources to prosecute criminal defendants for the crime, and then again for lying about it. But the privilege is not a component of fundamental fairness. It should not have been applied to the states under the Fourteenth Amendment's due process clause. It should not prevent jurors from drawing conclusions from a defendant's failure to testify. And it certainly should not be used, as *Miranda* has allowed it to be used, as a free stay-out-of-jail card by suspects who have not been "read their rights."

The Judicial Filibuster—Violating the Constitution as a Rule

The rules of the United States Senate allow debate on a matter to continue indefinitely unless and until 60 of the 100 senators vote to cut off debate. This talk-until-60-cows-come-home is called a filibuster. Democrats are filibustering a number of President Bush's judicial nominees, and they threaten to filibuster future judicial nominees who are unacceptable to them. Until a deal that allowed votes on judicial nominations to proceed under reduced threat of filibuster, Republicans were prepared to implement a strategy that would have required only 50 senators, plus Vice President Cheney as tie-breaker, to remove judicial confirmation debates from the filibuster rule, allowing any nominee to be confirmed if 51 senators supported him. The Republicans' characterized their strategy as the constitutional option, while Senate Democrats insisted that it was a nuclear option. Whatever it was called, it got people's attention.

When the Republican strategy was on the table, both sides, like Claw-fingered Kitty and Windy Ike in one of Robert Service's poems, fanged-up like dogs at bay, with partisans on both sides using money, media, rallies, intense political pressure and the blogosphere to make their case. The Republicans claimed that, while there was no stated exception to the filibuster rule for judicial confirmation votes, the filibuster had never been used against judicial nominees, and its use against nominees was not permitted by the Constitution. The Democrats countered that judicial nominees had in fact been filibustered, and that the right to filibuster was as American as baseball, hot dogs, apple pie and Chevrolet and was consistent with the Constitution's focus on minority rights and balance of power between the executive and legislative branches.

I don't know how the filibuster stacks up against baseball, hot dogs, apple pie and Chevrolet. I also don't know whether the filibuster had ever been used to block judicial nominees before the Democrats made widespread use of it during George W. Bush's first term, although the Democrats did not cite a single instance in which the filibuster had been used to block the confirmation of a nominee who had majority support in the Senate. It is clear, however, that a judicial filibuster cannot find refuge in minority rights or separation of power doctrines enshrined in the Constitution. On the contrary, the Constitution requires an expeditious 50 percent up or down vote on judicial and other presidential nominees.

The roles of the president and the Senate in the appointment of judges and government officials are set forth in Article II, Section 2 of the Constitution, which states that the president "shall have the power, by and with the advice and consent of the Senate, to make treaties, provided two thirds of the senators present shall concur; and he shall nominate, and by and with the advice and consent of the Senate, shall appoint ambassadors, other public ministers and consuls, judges of the Supreme Court, and all other officers of the United States..." Since this provision requires a two thirds vote to ratify a treaty but only a simple advice and consent for confirmation of judges and executive officials, the Constitution clearly contemplates a simple majority vote for confirmation.

Democrats justify the judicial filibuster rule under Article I, Section 5 of the Constitution, which authorizes each House of Congress "to determine the rules of its proceedings." This provision, they say, allows the Senate to adopt and universally apply a rule to block majority votes by requiring a supermajority vote to cut off debate.

Article I of the Constitution establishes the legislative power of Congress, and Congress can of course adopt such rules as it chooses for conduct of that business. But when the Senate joins in the presidential appointment process under Article II, Section 2 it is not conducting legislative business

Article II, Section 2 establishes powers of the president, not powers of Congress. The president is authorized to nominate judges and executive officials, and then to appoint them "by and with the advice and consent of the Senate." The Senate is given the power to approve or reject nominees, to be sure, but it primarily plays a supporting role, instructed to facilitate presidential appointments. This role demands expeditious and dispositive Senate consideration of presidential nominees, as confirmed not only by the president-supporting nature of the role, but also by the recess appointment provisions of Section 2. These provisions give the president unilateral power to fill vacancies that "may happen" during a recess of the Senate, with the recess appointment to expire at the end of the next Senate session. These provisions obviously assume that the Senate will act on an appointment during the session in which the appointment is made. And as we have seen, the Constitution requires the Senate to act by majority, not supermajority, vote. When applied to presidential nominees, the Senate's supermajority filibuster rule ignores the role of the Senate in the appointment process and spurns the Constitution's demand that the Senate act expeditiously and by majority action. The rule is unconstitutional.

Some conservatives want to hoard the judicial filibuster for the day the Democrats regain control of the Senate and White House. But even if conservatives were inclined to sacrifice constitutional principle to pragmatism, they would sacrifice in vain. The liberal vision of the Constitution is the entrenched law of the land. No matter where he or she stood in the spectrum of the left, a Democrat Supreme Court nominee would vote to uphold this vision. Republicans could not filibuster until they found a nominee prepared to change the law. If conservatives get to define constitutional law for the next 60 years, as liberals have for the last 60, they too could be nonchalant about Supreme Court appointments.

Democrats not only claim that Senate legislative rules can be used to gum up the appointment process. They also argue that the Constitution contemplates presidential consultation with the Senate before a nomination is made.

This is demonstrably false. Article II, Section 2 states that the president "shall nominate, and by and with the advice and consent of the Senate, shall appoint." First comes the nomination, and *then* the advice and consent. This reading is confirmed by Alexander Hamilton in *Federalist 76*, where he says in speaking of the president's role under the appointment provisions that "in the act of nomination, his judgment alone would be exercised."

The Democrats should return to the practice of centuries, using the filibuster in the legislative but not the appointment process. Custom commends it, and the Constitution demands it.

CHAPTER 8

Conclusion: Speaking Power to Untruth

When the constitutional worm turned in the late 1930s, one of the Four Horsemen—the quartet of Justices Butler, McReynolds, Van Devanter and Sutherland who brought down a flock of state and federal laws regulating economic activities—exclaimed that "the Constitution, it is gone!" It was not gone then, of course, as the long assault on the Constitution detailed in this book had only just begun, and even now it is an overstatement to say that the Constitution is gone, but several of the Constitution's most important provisions have been unconstitutionally amended by the Supreme Court. It will not be easy to steer those provisions back to their constitutional port.

Only two of the thirteen Supreme Court justices appointed since 1967 have been appointed by a Democrat president, and at all times since 1972 Republican appointees have constituted a majority of the Court's members. Yet despite an occasional nick here and there, the liberal legacy of the Roosevelt and Warren Courts has not only survived, but has thrived and expanded. Why?

In part it's because Republican presidents made mistakes. Republican appointees Blackmun, Stevens and Souter were either liberals from the start or headed left within a short time after their appointments, and Brennan, who served until 1990, was a known liberal Democrat when Eisenhower appointed him in 1956. In part it's because a few Democrat appointees hung on for a while. Douglas served until 1975, Marshall until 1990, White until 1993. Mostly, though, it's because Republican appointees like Chief Justice Warren Burger and Justices O'Connor, Kennedy and Lewis Powell, generally conservative in outlook, were sucked into the judicial mainstream.

The Supreme Court's decisions, while liberal in outcome, reflect a conservative process and approach to decision-making. Justices are led to believe that the Court's standing and legitimacy demand consistency, continuity and respect for precedent. Strong centripetal forces pull justices to acceptance and expansion of the judicial mainstream. Recently, only Rehnquist, Scalia and Thomas have managed to stay out of the water, although it appears likely that they will be joined by Roberts and Alito.

The Supreme Court's mainstream is now far from its constitutional channel. It will take difficult, extensive judicial engineering to restore the stream to its channel. Bush has had two Supreme Court appointees. With ultra-liberal Justice John Paul Stevens turning 88 well before the end of Bush's term, Bush may have at least one more appointment. To provide the needed engineering, the Bush appointees will have to ignore false appeals to the Court's reputation and standing and withstand full-blooded, well-funded attacks from liberal media, constituencies and activists. They will need the self-assurance, convictions and confidence necessary to speak power to untruth. If they do so, they can re-channel the judicial mainstream to a bed rooted in the Constitution, making it difficult for future liberal justices to ignore and amend the Constitution. If they fail to do so, they will allow the liberals to lay waste to the Constitution for another generation or more, with damage so long-lasting and extensive that it can probably never be repaired.

APPENDIX

Selected Provisions of the Constitution

Preamble

We the people of the United States, in order to form a more perfect union, establish justice, insure domestic tranquility, provide for the common defence, promote the general welfare, and secure the blessings of liberty to ourselves and our posterity, do ordain and establish this Constitution for the United States of America.

Article I, Section 8. Congressional powers.

The Congress shall have power to lay and collect taxes, duties, imposts and excises, to pay the debts and provide for the common defence and general welfare of the United States; but all duties, imposts and excises shall be uniform throughout the United States;

To borrow money on the credit of the United States;

To regulate commerce with foreign nations, and among the several states, and with the Indian tribes;

To establish an uniform rule of naturalization, and uniform laws on the subject of bankruptcy throughout the United States;

To coin money, regulate the value thereof, and of foreign coin, and fix the standard of weights and measures;

To provide for the punishment of counterfeiting the securities and current coin of the United States;

To establish post offices and post roads;

To promote the progress of science and useful arts, by securing for limited times to authors and inventors the exclusive right to their respective writings and discoveries;

To constitute tribunals inferior to the supreme court;

To define and punish piracies and felonies committed on the high seas, and offences against the law of nations;

To declare war, grant letters of marque and reprisal, and make rules concerning captures on land and water;

To raise and support armies, but no appropriation of money to that use shall be for a longer term than two years;

To provide and maintain a navy;

To make rules for the government and regulation of the land and naval forces;

To provide for calling forth the militia to execute the laws of the union, suppress insurrections and repel invasions;

To provide for organizing, arming, and disciplining, the militia, and for governing such part of them as may be employed in the service of the United States, reserving to the states respectively, the appointment of the officers, and the authority of training the militia according to the discipline prescribed by Congress;

To exercise exclusive legislation in all cases whatsoever, over such district (not exceeding ten miles square) as may, by cession of particular states, and the acceptance of congress, become the seat of the government of the United States, and to exercise like authority over all places purchased by the consent of the legislature of the state in which the same shall be, for the erection of forts, magazines, arsenals, dock-yards, and other needful buildings;—and

To make all laws which shall be necessary and proper for carrying into execution the foregoing powers, and all other powers vested by this constitution in the government of the United States, or in any department or officer thereof.

Article II, Section 2. Presidential powers

The president shall be commander in chief of the army and navy of the United States, and of the militia of the several states, when called into the actual service of the United States; he may require the opinion, in writing, of the principal officer in each of the executive departments, upon any subject relating to the duties of their respective offices, and he shall have power to grant reprieves and pardons for offences against the United States, except in cases of impeachment.

He shall have power, by and with the advice and consent of the senate, to make treaties, provided two thirds of the senators present concur; and he shall nominate, and by and with the advice and consent of the senate, shall appoint ambassadors, other public ministers and consuls, judges of the supreme court, and all other officers of the United States, whose appointments are not otherwise herein provided for, and which shall be established by law; but the congress may by law vest the appointment of such inferior officers, as they think proper, in the president alone, in the courts of law, or in the heads of departments.

The president shall have power to fill up all vacancies that may happen during the recess of the senate, by granting commissions which shall expire at the end of the next session.

Article V. The amending provisions.

The congress, whenever two thirds of both Houses shall deem it necessary, shall propose amendments to this constitution, or, on the application of the legislatures of two thirds of the several states, shall call a convention for proposing amendments, which, in either case, shall be valid to all intents and purposes as part of this constitution, when ratified by the legislatures of three fourths of the several states, or by conventions in three fourths thereof, as the one or the other mode of ratification shall be proposed by the congress; provided that...no state, without its consent, shall be deprived of its equal suffrage in the senate.

Article VI, third paragraph. The constitutional oath.

The senators and representatives before mentioned, and the members of the several state legislatures, and all executive and judicial officers, both of the United States and of the several states, shall be bound by oath or affirmation, to support this constitution; but no religious test shall ever be required as a qualification to any office or public trust under the United States.

Bill of Rights. The first ten amendments.

First. Congress shall make no law respecting an establishment of religion, or prohibiting the free exercise thereof; or abridging the freedom of speech, or of the press; or the right of the people peaceably to assemble, and to petition congress for a redress of grievances.

Second. A well-regulated militia, being necessary to the security of a free state, the right of the people to keep and bear arms, shall not be infringed.

Third. No soldier shall, in time of peace be quartered in any house, without the consent of the owner, nor in time of war, but in a manner to be prescribed by law.

Fourth. The right of the people to be secure in their persons, houses, papers, and effects, against unreasonable searches and seizures, shall not be violated, and no warrants shall issue, but upon probable cause, supported by oath or affirmation, and particularly describing the place to be searched, and the persons or things to be seized.

Fifth. No person shall be held to answer for a capital or otherwise infamous crime, unless on a presentment or indictment of a grand jury, except in cases arising in the land or naval forces, or in the militia, when in actual service in time of war or public danger; nor shall any person be subject for the same offence to be twice put in jeopardy of life or limb; nor shall be compelled in any criminal case to be a witness against himself, nor be deprived of life, liberty or property, without due process of law; nor shall private property be taken for public use, without just compensation.

Sixth. In all criminal prosecutions, the accused shall enjoy the right to a speedy and public trial, by an impartial jury of the state and district wherein the crime shall have been committed, which district shall have been previously ascertained by law, and to be informed of the nature and cause of the accusation; to be confronted with the witnesses against him; to have compulsory process for obtaining witnesses in his favor, and to have assistance of counsel for his defence.

Seventh. In suits at common law, where the value in controversy shall exceed twenty dollars, the right of trial by jury shall be preserved, and no fact tried by a jury, shall be otherwise re-examined in any court of the United States, than according to the rules of the common law.

Eighth. Excessive bail shall not be required, nor excessive fines imposed, nor cruel and unusual punishments inflicted.

Ninth. The enumeration in the constitution, of certain rights, shall not be construed to deny or disparage others retained by the people.

Tenth. The powers not delegated to the United States by the constitution, nor prohibited by it to the states, are reserved to the states respectively, or to the people.

Fourteenth Amendment, Section 1. The due process clause.

All persons born or naturalized in the United States, and subject to the jurisdiction thereof, are citizens of the United States and of the state wherein they reside. No state shall make or enforce any law which shall abridge the privileges or immunities of citizens of the United States; nor shall any state deprive any person of life, liberty, or property, without due process of law; nor deny to any person within its jurisdiction the equal protection of the law.

Notes

Chapter 1—Original Meaning and Precedent

[1]. 17 U.S. 316 (1819)

[2]. 17 U.S. at 421

[3]. *Home Building and Loan Association v. Blaisdell*, 290 U.S. 398, 426 (l934)

[4]. *Federalist 41*

[5]. 330 U.S. 1 (1947)

[6]. 492 U.S. 573 (1989)

[7]. 381 U.S. 479 (1965)

[8]. 410 U.S. 113 (1973)

[9]. 505 U.S. 833 (1992)

[10]. In a withering attack in "The Wages of Crying Wolf: a Comment on *Roe v. Wade*," 82 *Yale Law Journal* 920 (1973), John Hart Ely, a liberal law professor and former law clerk for Chief Justice Earl Warren, said the opinion in *Roe* was bad "because it is not constitutional law and gives almost no sense of an obligation to try to be." In *Supreme Injustice* (New York: Oxford University Press, 2001), p. 194, liberal Harvard Law School Professor Alan M. Dershowitz, after discussing the extent to which *Roe* had distorted American politics, rejected *Roe* with the observation that "courts ought not to jump into controversies that are political in nature and are capable of being resolved by the popular branches of government." In *American Constitutional Law* (Mineola, New York: Foundation Press, 2nd Ed. 1988), p. 1351, ultra liberal Harvard Law School Professor Laurence Tribe, after detailing with seeming

approval all of the arguments that have been advanced against *Roe,* summarizes his verdict on *Roe* by saying that "although the matter is by far the most troublesome in constitutional law, the result in the abortion decision *seems defensible on other grounds.*" (Emphasis added.) And before she was appointed to the Supreme Court, liberal justice Ruth Bader Ginsburg said that *Roe* "halted a political process that was moving in a reform direction." See Charles Krauthammer's column in the April 22, 2005 *Washington Post.*

[11]. 60 U.S. 393 (1857)

[12]. *Ring v. Arizona,* 536 U.S. 584 (2002), overruling *Walton v. Arizona,* 497 U.S.639 (1990)

[13]. *Lawrence v. Texas,* 539 U.S. 558 (2003), overruling *Bowers v. Hardwick,* 478 U.S. 186 (1986)

[14]. *Roper v. Simmons,* 161 L. Ed. 2d 1(2005), overruling *Stanford v. Kentucky,* 492 U.S.361 (1989)

[15]. *Brown v. Board of Education,* 347 U.S. 483 (1954), overruling *Plessy v. Ferguson,* 163 U.S. 537 (1896), and a host of other cases

[16]. See chapters 2 and 3, detailing how the Supreme Court in 1937 ditched a long-standing line of property-friendly cases decided under the interstate commerce and due process clauses.

[17]. The most prominent example of jurisprudential reliance is major league baseball's antitrust exemption. In 1922, the Supreme Court, speaking through Justice Holmes, held that baseball was local commerce not subject to federal antitrust laws. *Federal Baseball Club of Baltimore, Inc. v. National Baseball Clubs,* 259 U.S. 200 (1922). Unconvincing even to conservatives, the economic analysis underpinning this decision has long since been abandoned by the Supreme Court,

but baseball's antitrust exemption lingers as a reliance-based beneficiary of Holmes' decision.

[18]. *Black and White Taxicab Co. v. Brown and Yellow Taxicab Co.*, 276 U.S. 518, 533 (1928)

Chapter 2. The Interstate Commerce Clause—Power Run Amok

[19] 22 U.S. 1 (1824)

[20]. *Shreveport Rate Cases*, 234 U.S. 342 (1914) (Interstate Commerce Act); *Hipolite Egg Co. v. United States*, 220 U.S. 45 (1911) (Food and Drug Act)

[21]. *Northern Securities Co. v. United States*, 193 U.S. 197 (1904); *Standard Oil Co. Of New Jersey v. United States*, 221 U.S. 1 (1911)

[22]. *Carter v. Carter Coal Co.*, 298 U.S. 238 (1936) (wages and hours); *Hammer v. Dagenhart*, 247 U.S. 251 (1918) (child labor)

[23]. *United States v. E.C. Knight Co.*, 156 U.S. 1 (1895)

[24]. See Chapter 1, footnote 17

[25]. *NLRB v. Jones & Laughlin Steel Corp.*, 301 U.S. 1 (1931)

[26]. 312 U.S. 100 (1941)

[27]. For the ranking of Jackson and other justices referred to in this book, see Henry J. Abraham, *Justices and Presidents* (New York: Oxford University Press, 3rd Ed. 1992), Appendix A.

[28]. 317 U.S. 111 (1942)

[29]. *Heart of Atlanta Motel v. United States*, 379 U.S. 241 (1964)

[30]. *Katzenbach v. McClung*, 379 U.S. 294 (1964)

[31]. *United States v. Lopez*, 514 U.S. 549 (1995); *United States v. Morrison*, 529 U.S. 598 (2000)

[32]. *Gibbs v. Babbitt*, 214 F. 3rd 483 (4th Cir. 2000)

[33]. *National Association of Homebuilders v. Babbitt*, 130 F 3rd 1041 (D.C. Cir. 1997)

[34]. *Andrus v. Allard*, 444 U.S. 51 (1979)

[35]. *United States v. Lewis*, 100 F. 3rd 49 (7th Cir. 1996)

[36]. *Russell v. United States*, 471 U.S. 858 (1985)

[37]. *United States v. Allen*, 341 F. 3rd 870 (9th Cir. 2003)

[38]. *United States v. Bramble*, 103 F. 3rd 1475 (9th Cir. 1996)

Chapter 3. The Due Process Clause—Legislators in Robes

[39]. 83 U.S. 36 (1873)

[40]. 94 U.S. 113 (1877)

[41]. 116 U.S. 307 (1886)

[42]. 165 U. S. 578 (1897)

[43]. 198 U. S. 45 (1905)

[44]. *Coppage v. Kansas*, 236 U.S. 1 (1915)

[45]. *Truax v. Corrigan*, 257 U.S. 312 (1921)

[46]. *Morehead v. New York ex. rel. Tipaldo*, 298 U.S. 587 (1936)

[47]. *Tyson Brothers v. Banton*, 273 U.S. 418 (1927)

[48]. *New State Ice Co. v. Liebmann*, 285 U.S. 262 (1932)

[49]. *Adams v. Tanner*, 244 U.S. 590 (1917)

[50]. 300 U.S. 379 (1937)

[51]. 332 U.S. 46 (1947), Frankfurter concurring opinion at 332 U.S. at 66

[52]. 304 U.S. 144 (1938)

[53]. *Prudential Ins. Co. v. Cheek*, 259 U.S. 530, 543 (1922)

[54]. 274 U.S. 357 (1927)

[55]. 32 U.S. 243 (1833)

[56]. 211 U.S. 78 (1908)

[57]. 268 U.S. 652 (1925)

[58]. 287 U.S. 45 (1932)

[59]. See Erwin Chemerinsky, *Constitutional Law Principles and Policies* (New York: Aspen Publishers, 2nd Ed. 2002), pages 482-486.

[60]. Recognizing that Black's incorporation doctrine does not pass the laugh test, Yale Law School Professor Akhil Reed Amar resurrects the privileges and immunities clause, contending that it was designed to incorporate the Bill of Rights. Amar, *The Bill of Rights* (New Haven: Yale University Press, 1988). Amar's theory is so full of holes it's hard to know where to start.

Unlike the due process clause, which applies to all "persons," the privileges and immunities clause protects only "citizens," defined as persons born or naturalized in the United States. It excludes non-naturalized immigrants, whether legal or illegal. Contrast this not only to the due process clause, but to the Bill of Rights, which refers to "persons" twice and "people" three times, but never once mentions citizens. Why this difference, unless the privileges and immunities clause is designed, not to incorporate the grand, universal rights and liberties of the Bill of Rights, but only to protect rights peculiar to citizenship?

Each of the provisions of the Bill of Rights insulates Americans from federal exercise or abuse of power. Amar argues that these constitutional protections from federal power are "privileges and immunities of citizens of the United States" protected from state power under the privileges and immunities clause. As Hamilton notes in *Federalist 84*, the Constitution protects Americans from all powers not given to the federal government. If constitutional protection from federal power becomes immunity from state power under the privileges and immunities clause, as Amar contends, his approach would deprive the states of all non-federal powers, reducing them to mere carbon copies of the federal government and creating a monstrous power vacuum.

I could go on, but the main objection to Amar's notion that the privilege and immunities clause incorporates the Bill of Rights is the same as the main objection to Black's incorporation doctrine—if Congress had wanted to apply the rights to the states, it wouldn't do it this way. The privileges and immunities clause is designed to protect rights peculiar to citizenship, which is pretty much what Justice Miller said in the *Slaughter-House Cases*. Maybe that's why he's numbered among the Court's near great justices.

[61]. 332 U.S. at 62, 65.

[62]. *Callins v. Collins*, 510 U.S. 1141 (1994). For constitutional provisions acknowledging the power to impose the death penalty, see the due process clauses of the Fifth and Fourteenth Amendments, recognizing federal and state power to deprive people of life with due process of law, and the provision in the Fifth Amendment requiring indictment by a grand jury in any case in which the death penalty can be imposed.

Chapter 4. The Ungodly Abuse of the Establishment Clause

[63]. 545 U.S. 844 (2005)

[64]. 545 U.S. 677 (2005)

[65]. 536 U.S. 639 (2002)

[66]. This list is set forth in Justice Rehnquist's dissent in *Wallace v. Jaffree*, 472 U.S. 38, 110-111 (1985)

[67]. *Lemon v. Kurtzman*, 403 U.S. 602 (1971)

[68]. 379 U.S. 241 at 257

[69]. Leonard W. Levy, *The Establishment Clause: Religion and the First Amendment* (Chapel Hill, University of North

Carolina Press, 2nd Ed. 1994), p. 10. This book will be cited below as *The Establishment Clause.*

[70]. For a detailed history of establishments and disestablishments of religion in the United States, see *The Establishment Clause,* pages 1-78.

[71]. See *The Establishment Clause,* p. 70.

[72]. See Alan Kors and Harvey Silverglate, *The Shadow University: The Betrayal of Liberty on American Campuses* (New York: Harper, 1998), and the September, 2002 *American Enterprise Magazine.*

[73]. *The Establishment Clause,* p 148.

[74]. For a discussion of the Bill of Rights provisions that have and have not been applied to the states under the incorporation doctrine, see *Constitutional Law Principles and Policies,* cited above, pages 482-484.

[75]. 496 U.S. 226 at 260 (1990)

[76]. 472 U.S. 38 at 91 (1985)

[77]. This chapter is modified from an article that appeared in *American Experiment Quarterly,* vol. 5, no. 4 (2002).

Chapter 5. Bush and Gore in Florida—The Wait of the World

[78]. *Palm Beach Canvassing Board v. Harris,* 772 So. 2nd 1220 (2000)

[79]. *Bush v. Palm Beach Canvassing Board,* 531 U.S. 70 (2000)

[80]. *Gore v. Harris,* 772 So. 2nd 1243 (2000)

[81]. *Bush v. Gore,* 531 U.S. 98 (2000)

[82]. 405 U.S. 56 (1972)

[83]. *Supreme Injustice,* above, pages 95-172. For his speculation on the O'Connor and Rehnquist retirements and Kennedy's desire to be Chief Justice, see pages 156, 162 and 169.

[84]. *Supreme Injustice*, p. 194.

[85]. *Delahunt v. Johnston*, 671 N.E.2nd 1241 (1996)

[86]. This chapter is modified from an article that appeared in *American Experiment Quarterly*, vol. 4, no. 1 (2001).

Chapter 6. The Nature of the Union—Secession and States Rights

[87]. 426 U.S. 833 (1976)

[88]. 469 U.S. 528 (1985)

[89]. "Secession: A Constitutional Remedy for the Breach of the Organic Law," volume 3, number 6, p. 12.

[90]. In fact, many of the statements appear to apply to the Articles of Confederation rather than the Constitution, and many were made long after the adoption of the Constitution. In an 1821 letter which Brown cites, Madison refers to the Constitution as a "compact," but he was at the constitutional convention a "strong government" proponent who said that the difference between a government founded on legislatures and one founded on people is "the difference between a league or treaty and a constitution." Catherine Drinker Bowen, *Miracle at Philadelphia* (Boston: Little Brown, 1966), pages 225-226.

[91]. *Miracle at Philadelphia*, p. 42.

[92]. The debate on the basis for representation in Congress focused more on power than it did on states rights as an abstract concept. Virginia, one of the most strident champions of states rights after the Constitution was adopted, argued in convention for population-based representation in both houses of Congress. *Miracle at Philadelphia*, p. 84.

[93]. Article VII, which makes the Constitution effective upon ratification by nine states.

[94]. Article IV, Section 3, authorizing Congress to admit new states.

[95]. See, for example, the First Inaugural Address, in which Lincoln said that "in contemplation of...the Constitution, the Union of these states is perpetual," and Lincoln's November 9, 1863 letter to Benjamin Flanders, quoted at Roy Basler, *The Collected Works of Abraham Lincoln* (New Brunswick: Rutgers University Press, 1953), Volume VII, p. 6, in which Lincoln states that "I have always thought the act of secession is legally nothing, and needs no repealing."

[96]. Basler, Volume VIII, p. 403.

[97]. Eric Foner, *Reconstruction:America's Unfinished Revolution* (New York: Harper and Row, 1988), p. 230.

[98]. Constitution, Article IV, Section 3. Lincoln delivered an opinion on the constitutionality of West Virginia's admission. It is artful and ingenious, striving to find support in the Constitution but ultimately concluding that if West Virginia is unlawfully seceding from Virginia, "there is...difference enough between secession against the Constitution and secession in favor of the Constitution." Basler, Volume VI, pages 26-28.

[99]. See generally, *Reconstruction: America's Unfinished Revolution*, pages 271-280.

[100]. In *Texas v. White*, 74 U.S. 700 (1869), the Supreme Court held, in a fairly summary fashion, with little analysis, that secession was unconstitutional. The parties, however, were Texas and its bondholders, not the federal government, and by 1869 the federal government had, in any event, accomplished everything mentioned in the text.

[101]. 17 U.S. 316, at 429

[102].It is often said that the federal insulation from state power is required by Article VI of the Constitution, stating that "the constitution and laws of the United States...shall be the supreme law of the land." This is bogus. Subjecting the federal government to non-discriminatory taxes and building codes does not threaten the supremacy of federal laws or the Constitution. Marshall does in *McCulloch* mention the supremacy clause, but as the quoted language from *McCulloch* indicates, it is a lack of state power over the federal government, not the supremacy clause, that shields the federal government from the states.

Chapter 7. Grab Bag of Constitutional Shenanigans

[103].402 U.S. 183 (1971)
[104].408 U.S. 238 (1972)
[105].428 U.S. 280 (1976)
[106].497 U.S. 639 (1990)
[107].536 U.S. 584 (2002)
[108].492 U.S. 302 (1989)
[109].536 U.S. 304 (2002)
[110].492 U.S. 361 (1989)
[111].161 L. Ed. 2d 1(2005)
[112].428 U.S. 52 (1976)
[113].539 U.S. 224 (2003)
[114].539 U.S. 306 (2003)
[115].211 U.S. 78, at 113(1908)
[116].*Palko v. Connecticut*, 302 U.S. 319, at 326(1937)
[117].*Adamson v. California*, 332 U.S. 46, at 59-60(1947)
[118].*Malloy v. Hogan*, 378 U.S. 1 (1964)
[119].*Griffin v. California*, 380 U.S. 609 (1965)
[120].384 U.S. 436 (1966)

Index

Harlan, John Marshall II 159

Harriman, Edward 43

Havemeyer, Henry 43, 45

Heart of Atlanta Motel v. United States 48, 100, n.29

Henry, Patrick 38

Hill, James J. 43

Hipolite Egg Co. v. United States n.20

Holmes, Oliver Wendell, Jr. 14, 30, 33-34, 45, 46, 49, 69, 76, 79, 84, 92, 98, n.17

Home Building and Loan Association v. Blaisdell n.3

Hughes, Charles Evans 19, 69-70, 77, 84

Humphrey, Hubert 23, 155

Incorporation doctrine 65, 75, 87, 92, 110
    Absurdity of 78-79
    Analyzed and criticized 76-77, 78-80
    Defined 79

Interstate Commerce Act 44

Interstate commerce clause. See Commerce clause

Jackson, Jesse 129